SUPERNATURAL ST

SUPERNATURAL
ST ANDREWS

A Guide to the Town's Dark History, Ghosts and Ghouls

Gregor Stewart

GREGOR STEWART

All rights reserved. This book, or parts thereof, may not be reproduced or transmitted in any form or by any means, electronic or mechanical, including printing, recording, photocopying or by any information storage and retrieval system without written permission from the author.

Unless otherwise states, all photographs and illustrations are either taken from the author's personal collection or are sourced from online encyclopaedias and are believed to be in the public domain

This book is written in British English

© G Stewart 2015

HAUNTED PUBLISHING

CONTENTS

About the Author
Introduction
The Old Course to the Castle
The Cathedral, the Pends and the Harbour
The Town Centre
Further Afield
Additional Information and Other Publications
Bibliography

The St Andrews Coat of Arms

SUPERNATURAL ST ANDREWS

ABOUT THE AUTHOR

Before I share the ghost stories from St Andrews and the surrounding area, it is probably appropriate to give a little information about myself. I was raised in the 1970s in the town of St Andrews in Fife, a town that is considered to be one of the most haunted locations in Scotland, a country that is considered to be one of the most haunted countries in the world and so, from a young age, I have been surrounded by tales of ghosts and mysterious places. My grandfather, who was a painter by trade, but who was also a specialist in fine gold leaf detailing, initially fired my interest in the supernatural. His gold leaf work led him to work on some of the most prestigious buildings in the area, such as the historic buildings of St Andrews University, the oldest university in Scotland and third oldest in the UK, and also nearby Falkland Palace, the former country retreat of the Stuart Monarchs, where he was involved with the restoration of the king's bedroom and the chapel. While carrying out work in buildings such as these, he used to hear some of the ghostly tales connected with them that he would pass on to me.

When the time came for me to be considered old enough by my parents to get a weekly comic (which was quite a normal thing in the 70s and 80s), rather than choosing one of the traditional comics such as the Beano or the Dandy, I opted for a new magazine that was about to be released by Orbis Publishing which was entitled The Unexplained: Mysteries of Time, Space and Mind and while my friends were making their weekly trips to the local newsagent to collect the latest edition of tales of mischief from the likes of Dennis the Menace and Minnie the Minx, I was eager to get my hands on the next copy of what many considered to be my 'weird magazine', so that I could read the next instalment of the stories of ghosts, monsters and myths. The Unexplained was published from 1980 until 1983, with over one hundred and fifty magazines that combined to make a series of encyclopaedias, which I have read from cover to cover and that I still own and refer to today.

As I grew older, my interest also grew, particularly in the reports of haunted locations, and I started to purchase as many books on ghost stories from around the world as I could. I also took every opportunity to visit old houses and castles to hear the tales and experience the atmosphere of these buildings myself, which is something I continued to do into adulthood and, some forty years later, I still do today. Over the years, this has allowed me to build up a fairly extensive library of ghost and history books with publication dates ranging from the 1800s to the present day. I also have a collection of hundreds of photographs from the many locations I have visited.

My interest in old buildings extends beyond reputedly haunted locations, I admire them for their history and architecture as well, and so, while I frequently visit locations that I know have ghostly tales attached to them, I equally visit places where I am neither aware of, nor looking for, any associated stories of the paranormal, I am simply looking at the building to explore and appreciate the historic significance. Even so, I am rarely without a camera and a digital voice recorder and I always take a lot of photographs and, every now and again, something I can't quite explain shows up in the photos or I am told a story of local folklore or personal experience by those who look after the properties, prompting an unplanned investigation.

I don't consider myself to have any real psychic abilities, but I do believe I have a high level of intuition. I can generally read people quite easily and often get a gut feeling when something is going to happen, and it then does. This carries across to when I am visiting a place and I just get a feeling that something is not as it appears to be. That said, I still remain an open-minded sceptic. I am frequently asked the question 'do you believe in ghosts?' and my answer is always the same, 'no'. This frequently surprises people who I have previously spoken to passionately about haunted locations but, until such time as I experience something that will prove to me without a doubt that ghosts exist, I cannot state that I believe in them. For the same reasons however, I equally cannot say that I disbelieve in the existence of ghosts! My attitude is never to jump to conclusions and to keep an open mind.

During my years of visiting these historic locations I have taken numerous photographs which reveal unusual lights, recorded disembodied voices replying to questions I have asked during investigations, witnessed the sound of footsteps from empty rooms and corridors, heard the slam of heavy doors being closed with considerable force in a building where no doors remain and I have had personal information relayed to me via a Ouija board session but, just because I cannot explain any of these incidents, it doesn't mean I will conclude that it was ghosts that were causing them. They are, and remain, simply unexplained experiences.

My hope is to one day find out what does cause incidents such as these as I do believe there is something out there, something we do not fully understand, but I do not know what....not yet! An anonymous historian who has been quoted in several early publications tells us that 'truth is in folklore, you'll not find lies carried down the years', and that is a statement that I fully believe in. It fascinates me that these stories have been passed down from generation to generation and that they still survive today, to be passed onto future generations. In addition, the sheer number of people who claim to have encountered similar things in similar locations over the years also, to me, adds to the validity. I do also however believe that as the stories have been passed on they have no doubt been embellished to increase their dramatic effect or to suit slightly different circumstances and so I feel it is important to look back to try to find the origins of the story, wherever possible. In researching the stories for this book this is something that I have tried to do and, where there is no or limited written documentation, I have attempted to speak directly to those who are today connected with the buildings or locations.

In addition to this title, I have written 'Haunted Kirkcaldy', published by the History Press, and two series of books, the first being the 'Haunted Explorer' series which, starting with the book 'Scotland's Hidden Hauntings', covers many haunted locations throughout Scotland. My fictional 'Witch Hunter' series, starting with 'Rise of the Witch', tells the story of a powerful witch from the past being reborn in today's world and the battle the authorities have to bring her campaign of destruction to an end in a society that no longer believes in magic.

INTRODUCTION

The town of St. Andrews is known world-wide as the home of golf however, as well as housing the governing body of golf at the Royal and Ancient Golf Club, which overlooks the 1st tee and 18th hole of the Old Course, St. Andrews has far more to offer. It is the place where the bones of Andrew the Apostle, who would become the Patron Saint of the country, first landed on Scottish soil, and it was a major religious centre with a large, prestigious cathedral, the ruins of which, described by Historic Scotland as the 'remains of medieval Scotland's largest and most magnificent church', can still be explored today. The town also boasts the ruins of an impressive castle, once home to Scotland's leading bishop, and later archbishops, throughout the middle ages, in addition to the country's oldest university which, having been founded in 1413, is also the third oldest university in the English speaking world and today is a place where ordinary people can mix with the rich and famous, or even royalty. St Andrews is also home to one other thing....ghosts, and there are plenty of them!

The skyline of St Andrews from the sea

When considering the history of the town, it is perhaps not surprising to learn that there are reports of many locations being haunted. As the religious capital of the country, pilgrims were attracted from far and wide, and when the reformation came to Scotland, the town witnessed more violence than most in the vicious power struggles between the religious factions that would leave the once dominant city in ruins for over a century until the historical importance of the area was once again recognised and restoration work to attract visitors helped turn around the towns fortunes. It should not be surprising to learn that many of the ghosts of St Andrews are in some way connected to religion, which fortunately brings the advantage of historical records being available to provide at least some verification of the incidents that lead to the hauntings and, with the first religious settlement being established in the area in the year 370, there is plenty of history to pick from.

In this collection of the town's ghost stories, I have brought together the tales of the famous spooks and many of those that are less well known, along with the historical details behind the hauntings and, wherever possible, I have sourced early recordings of sightings of the spirits that are said to still walk the town today. The extensive photographs will assist the reader to visualise the locations, and the tales have been purposely set out to follow certain routes through the town, with maps to assist, to allow any visitors to use the book as a guide to explore for themselves.

The famous Swilcan Bridge, part of a larger painting by my late grandfather

THE OLD COURSE TO THE CASTLE

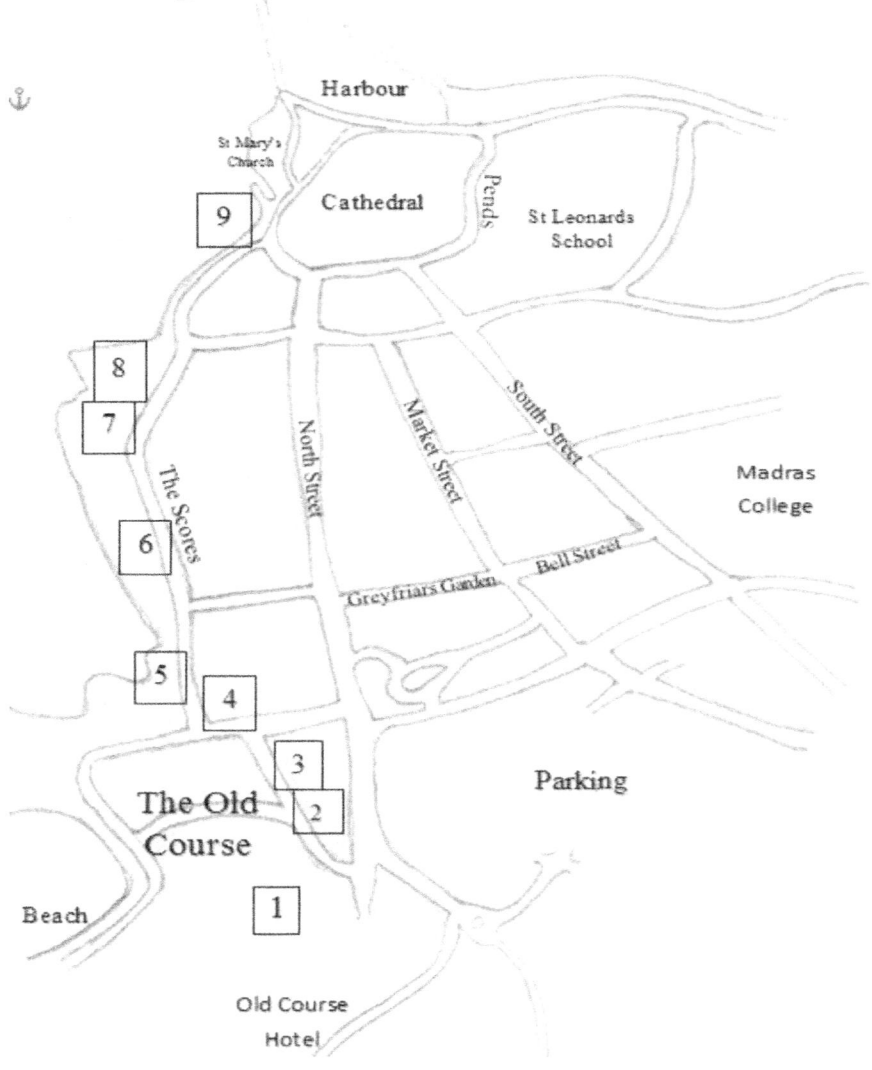

1) The Old Course
2) Rusacks Hotel
3) Links House
4) Hamilton Grand
5) Witch Hill & Lake
6) The Principals House
7) Castlecliffe
8) The Castle
9) Lady Buchanan's Cave

THE OLD COURSE

As you approach St Andrews from the west, you get your first glimpse of one of the most famous locations in the town, the Old Course. People have been playing golf in this area, known as the links, since the early 1400s, until, in 1457, King James II of Scotland banned golf due to an increasing concern that too many young men were turning their backs on other sports, such as archery, which was considered to give essential skills for war at a time when raids and battles were never far away. In 1502, King James IV lifted the ban, and fifty years later, in 1552, the people of St Andrews were formally granted the right to play golf on the links, officially establishing the course now known as the Old Course.

The Old Course

The current course was largely saved and redesigned by a local man named Tom Morris, a golfing icon not just for his skills in course design but also as club and ball maker, golf tutor and as a player, with him winning the open championship in 1861, 1862, 1864 and 1867. He still holds the record for being the oldest winner of the Open Championship at 46 years old and amazingly continued playing in the competition every year until 1895 when, at the ripe old age of 74, he decided to no longer compete.

Sadly, despite the fame, respect and success that Old Tom (as he was affectionately known) achieved, his personal life was full of tragedy. Tom married a local woman named Agnes Bayne in 1844, and they went onto have five children. Old Tom was to outlive them all. Possibly, the most tragic loss was of his son, Tommy (also known as Young Tom Morris). Tommy, like his father, became a very successful golfer, winning his first Open Championship in 1868, aged just 17, the youngest player ever to have won it. Old Tom finished second in the same competition, securing their position as top players of the time. Tommy went on to win the next three championships, making him the first player to ever win four consecutive Open Championships, a feat no other golfer since has managed to achieve.

Old and Young Tom Morris circa 1870-1875

As well as being a successful player in his own right, Tommy often teamed up with his father, forming a formidable pairs team. It was while doing so, playing in North Berwick on 4th September 1875, that he received the news that would ultimately lead to his demise. Tommy's wife, Margaret, was heavily pregnant and had not been keeping well. With the baby due imminently, it is said Tommy wanted to stay at home in St Andrews to look after her, but she persuaded him to go with his father to play in the competition. During the game, a telegram was received saying Margaret was in childbirth and requesting that Tommy returned home immediately. There are conflicting versions of exactly what happened with the telegram, with some versions of the story saying that it was handed to Old Tom close to the end of the game who realised that if Tommy knew, he would want to leave immediately resulting in them forfeiting the game (and losing the prize money). As they were close to winning, and he knew they would have to wait for the train back to St Andrews anyway and so little could be gained by leaving immediately, he chose to not say anything until after the game (which they went on to win). Other versions state that the telegram was delivered directly to Tommy just after the game. With Tommy anxious to return home, a Good Samaritan offered to take them back to St Andrews by boat, which would be far quicker.

Unfortunately, when they arrived they were given the sad news that both Margaret and the baby had died. Tommy was understandably devastated and he never got over his loss. A few months later, on Christmas Day, Old Tom found Tommy dead in his room. Whenever Old Tom heard anyone comment that Tommy had died of a broken heart, he is said to have responded that he did not believe that was the case as, if it was, he would also be dead, which gave an indication of the burden and guilt Old Tom carried for the rest of his life.

Old Tom's own death in 1908 was as a result of a terrible accident. While in the New Golf Club, which overlooks the Old Course, he fell down the stairs to the basement and never recovered from his injuries. It is believed he had mistaken the door to the basement for the door to the toilet.

> TOM MORRIS 1821-1908
> OLD TOM WON THE OPEN
> FOUR TIMES (1861-62, 1864, 1867),
> A FEAT MATCHED BY HIS SON,
> TOMMY (1868-70, 1872).
> THE FATHER OF MODERN
> GREEN-KEEPING, HE WAS KEEPER
> OF THE GREEN AT PRESTWICK
> AND AT ST ANDREWS (1864-1903);
> A PIONEER OF PROFESSIONAL
> GOLF; AND A PROLIFIC GOLF
> COURSE DESIGNER.
> "THE GRAND OLD MAN OF GOLF"
> WAS INSTRUMENTAL IN THE
> FOUNDATION OF THE NEW GOLF
> CLUB (1902) AND WAS ITS FIRST
> HONORARY MEMBER. A REGULAR
> VISITOR, HE DIED ON 24TH MAY
> SHORTLY AFTER A TRAGIC FALL
> IN THIS CLUBHOUSE.
> FATHER AND SON ARE BURIED IN
> ST ANDREWS CATHEDRAL.

Plaque on New Golf Club Wall

With Old Tom's strong connection to the Old Course, and the circumstances surrounding his death, it would be easy to think that his spirit may still linger, and many people believe that he does so. His ghost is said to have been seen on the Old Course, particularly at the 18th green, which Old Tom designed and is in front of the workshop where he designed and sold his clubs.

It has also been said that the phantom figure of an old man with a heavy beard has been seen by students in the Hamilton Halls, a former student residence that will be covered in more detail later in this book. The distinctive beard has led to speculation that this figure may also be Old Tom, who frequented the building when it was a hotel.

Young Tom is also said to remain on the Old Course, with reports of him being seen in the rough, which seems odd as these are areas of the course he is unlikely to have spent any time in during his playing years! Frustratingly, although there are frequent mentions of the ghosts of both old and young Tom on the course, I can find no definitive record of witnesses giving details or dates and times of the sightings. It is possible these ghosts are more due to expectation rather than being actual hauntings.

There is another tale of an encounter with a far less friendly ghoul on the Old Course that has led to the belief in a bad luck omen amongst the golfing community. According to the legend, Archibald Montgomerie, the 13th Earl of Eglington, was playing golf on the Old Course on 4th October 1861, when he suddenly stopped and announced he could no longer continue playing. When asked why, he replied that he had just seen the Bodach Glas for a third time, which would surely mean something bad was going to happen. In Folklore, the Bodach Glas is a spirit that appears in the form of a tall, dark grey man. Seeing the figure is deemed, by some, to be a death omen, and it seems that the Earl certainly believed that to be the case. Whether his previous sightings were also on the Old Course, or at some earlier time at another location is not known (it is said he foretold the death of his wife a year earlier, at the age of just 32, and so this may have been related to a previous encounter with the spirit). That evening, the Earl died suddenly at Mount Melville House on the outskirts of St Andrews, aged 49.

Although the Bodach Glas in this tale would appear to be connected to the Earl's family, it is a tradition now that seeing a grey, or grey haired man, on the Old Course is a sign of bad luck. Anyone who frequents this area will however know that the sea mist can sweep in over the links quite quickly, shrouding everything in grey, and that it is also not unusual to see more elderly gentlemen playing a round of golf on the course. It would therefore appear to me that this tradition is more a convenient excuse to be used by golfers when they are having a particularly bad round, rather than an indication that the Bodach Glas still roams the course.

THE RUSACKS HOTEL, THE LINKS

The road that runs along the side of the 18th fairway of the Old Course is called the Links, which was no doubt named after the area. The Rusacks Hotel sits around mid-point on the Links, providing magnificent views across both the 1st and 18th holes of the Old Course and to the sea beyond, making it a favoured destination for visiting golfers from all over the world.

The Rusacks Hotel

The impressive four storey, 'B' listed building first opened in 1887 as a purpose built hotel. Some small cottages were attached to the side, probably to provide staff accommodation although later possibly also used as additional guest accommodation. It was in one of these cottages that, in 1958, poltergeist activity was experienced. The case is rather curious, as it started in February 1958 in a local authority property in a street named Oaktree Avenue in Kirkcaldy, Fife, a town that sits just over twenty miles away from St Andrews. We are rather fortunate in that the occurrences were investigated and well documented by the Society for Psychical Research, an organisation established in 1882 with the aim to 'conduct organised scholarly research into human experiences that challenge contemporary scientific models'. I have explored this case in some detail previously and it is covered in full in my book 'Haunted Kirkcaldy'. The Oaktree Avenue incident was a classic poltergeist case, with activity starting suddenly and gradually building to become increasingly disruptive, always seemingly surrounding the family's twelve year old daughter. On the night of the 11th/12th September, 1958, six months after the disturbances started at Oaktree Avenue, they came to an end with a final show of strength when a heavy wardrobe and a chair were moved to the centre of an empty bedroom.

As soon as the activity ended in Kirkcaldy, it was reported to have started at the cottage attached to the Rusacks Hotel, where items began to be thrown by an unseen force. These included a thick leather belt, a salt cellar, two scarves and a book that were thrown across the bedroom, and a cup, a dish and an ink bottle that were thrown from the mantelpiece. These incidents were witnessed by three members of a dance group who were staying in the cottage at the time, however, they moved out on 14th September when the hotel closed for winter. Items had continued to be thrown throughout the two days the dance group members remained, although it is not known whether the activity continued after they had left or whether it stopped immediately.

It is difficult to say what would cause an alleged poltergeist to suddenly leave one property only to re-appear in another some distance away and, curiously, the activity started in St Andrews with around the same level of energy as it had in Kirkcaldy immediately before, so the spirit was not simply moving on and starting again. Instead, it would appear as though it was pulled from one property to another, mid-haunting. What could cause this is not likely to ever be known for sure, although in their paper published in September 1959, the Society for Psychical Research recorded that other documented incidents of poltergeist activity had started elsewhere at the same time as the Kirkcaldy case, such as one at Long Island, New York, on 3rd February 1958. Common features were noted with the cases that started in February 1958, such as the locations were all coastal and, at the time they started, unusually high tides were being encountered. Just after the poltergeist activity moved from Kirkcaldy to St Andrews in September 1958, there were high tides in St Andrews of a sufficient level for weather warnings to be issued. The high tide was early in the morning, when there was the shift in location for the activity. This led them to speculate that the movement of such ghostly activity could be associated with more extreme tidal activity.

The sea swell along the St Andrews Coastline

LINKS HOUSE, THE LINKS

Slightly further up the Links stands Links House, another grand building comprising of three storeys with an attic level and basement. This category 'C' listed building was constructed in the late nineteenth century as a private residence and it remained a home until 1932, when it was bought by St Andrews Golf Club for the grand sum of £2700 and converted to their club house, at a cost of another £2000. The club house was formally opened on 20th July, 1933.

Links House

One of the most impressive internal features of this building is the staircase, which rises through the centre of the building with large landings that lead all the way around the stair opening on each level, granting access to the principle rooms, and it is on this staircase that the ghost story I am about to recall began.

In my youth growing up in St Andrews, one of my friends had an uncle who worked in the golf club and he was allowed into the building whenever his uncle was on duty, although he was often sent upstairs to keep out of the way of the members and visitors. I would join him whenever I could, as it was quite a novelty being able to spend time in the likes of the billiards room of such an impressive building. My friend told me that, on one occasion, when he was alone and had been sent upstairs, as he climbed the staircase, he caught sight of a figure moving on a higher floor. This in itself would not be unusual, however, something didn't seem right. The figure, who appeared to be wearing some form of robe, moved silently from the central landing into one of the rooms that overlooks the Old Course. My friend continued up the stairs and purposely walked round the landing, past the open door he had seen the figure walk through, glancing in as he did so. Upon seeing no-one there, he turned and went back for a better look and, to his amazement, he found the room was completely empty. There were no other doors into the room and, with the open staircase, there was no way anyone could have left the room without him seeing them. He told his uncle what he had seen and he confirmed that the figure had been seen before, although little was known about who he was. Due to the apparent robe, my friend speculated that it was a monk and, at that age, I was happy to accept that without question. As I began to become more inquisitive about reports of the paranormal several years later, I started to become curious as to why a monk would be in the building. It had never been connected to religion, no earlier building had stood there and, even if there was a ghost monk connected with the land, that would not explain why he was now walking the upper floor of a building that was not there in his time.

While doing the research for this book, I made enquiries with the Golf Club and was advised that while there was knowledge of the reported ghost in the building, there had not been any recent sightings. I did also find a case reported in the newspaper archives that may shed some light on who this figure may be. On 5th January, 1916, *the Dundee Evening Telegraph* reported that Major H G Fenton Newall had died that morning at his residence, the Links House, St Andrews. It is said Major Newall had lived in St Andrews for 23 years (which indicates he may have been the first occupier of Links House) and that as well as a distinguished military career with the 3rd Battalion Lancaster Fusiliers, he was known to be a keen and active Mason, being an honorary member of the St Andrews Masonic Lodge and a Past Master at Rothesay on the Isle of Bute, provisional Grand Master of Argyll and Bute and holding several offices in the Grand Lodge of Scotland. In golfing, he was said to have been an outstanding figure on the golf links, as well as a respected member of the Royal and Ancient Golf Club, which he had joined when he moved to St Andrews.

The circumstances of Major Newall's death are unusual, in that it is reported that he had been observed suddenly falling backwards while looking out of his bedroom window. Medical assistance was summoned immediately, but he was found to already be dead. No cause of death is given.

Although it can only be speculation, it is fair to assume that Major Newall was no stranger to wearing robes, especially through his Masonic connection, something that clearly meant a lot to him. In addition, almost without a doubt his bedroom window would be at the front overlooking the Old Course. Many reported hauntings surround sudden and unexpected deaths, which certainly was the case with Major Newall, and many ghosts are said to return to a place that they had strong ties to in life, which it is reasonable to assume was the case for his home overlooking his beloved golf course and the Royal and Ancient Golf Club.

As stated earlier, I can only speculate, but if I had the opportunity to carry out an investigation in this building, the spirit of Major Newall would be at the top of my list to try to contact.

THE HAMILTON GRAND

At the end of the Links, on the corner of Golf Place and The Scores, stands one of the most distinctive buildings in the town. Built from red sandstone and with two domes on the roof, the Hamilton Grand stands out for miles around.

The Hamilton Grand

Originally constructed in 1894 as a hotel (named the Grand Hotel) to cater for the increasing visitor numbers to the town due to the growth of tourism, it also sought to set new industry standards for luxury, with it being the first building in Scotland to have compressed gas operated lifts and hot and cold running water in all bathrooms. This, along with the stunning location overlooking the Old Course, the beaches and the sea, allowed the Grand Hotel to operate very successfully, even attracting royal guests. During the Second World War, the hotel was requisitioned by the armed forces to be used for accommodation and training facilities.

In 1946 the hotel was released from military use and was extensively refurbished to provide dining for up to one hundred and fifty people, three lounges and a ballroom. It was however never again to operate as a hotel and was purchased by St Andrews University for student accommodation in 1949, when it was re-named the Hamilton Halls, after the man who commissioned the construction of the building, Thomas Hamilton. As an interesting side note, it is said that Thomas Hamilton had applied for membership at the Royal and Ancient Golf Club, but for an undisclosed reason his membership was refused. In response, he had the Grand Hotel built, which looks down over the Royal and Ancient, to dominate the skyline and draw attention from the golf club. This seems to have worked to a certain extent, with the building being the second most photographed in the world of golf, only beaten by (as you have probably guessed) the Royal and Ancient Golf Club.

The Royal and Ancient and the Hamilton Grand

In 2005, the university stunned the local community by announcing it was to sell the building, as it was considered that it no longer met the expectations of the modern student and did not meet the universities own standards. With much speculation about what would happen to the building, it was soon bought by a US based investment company for the reported sum of £20 million. Plans were agreed for the building to be converted into luxury apartments, which, complete with a heli-pad on the roof, were said to be aimed at the 'one percenters' (or the wealthiest people in the world). The building was to be operated as an exclusive residence club, where members would 'buy' the use of an apartment for a certain number of weeks per year, rather than have total ownership. Unfortunately, shortly after work started, the global credit crunch hit and the building was left abandoned and falling into an increasingly poor state of repair. In 2009, Herbert Kohler, the president of the Kohler Company, stepped in and saved the building. The Kohler Company already had strong ties with the town through their ownership of the Old Course Golf and Country Club, and after purchasing the Hamilton Halls, no expense was spared on the renovations, with essentially the entire interior of the building being taken out, with the exception of the central staircase, and it being rebuilt floor by floor to the highest standard. Today the building has been re-named the Hamilton Grand and comprises of 26 luxury apartments, as well as facilities for the public.

There have been stories of ghosts at the Hamilton Grand for many years, predominantly during the time it was in the ownership of the university. An elderly man has been witnessed in several locations that, as mentioned earlier, many believe may be the spirit of Old Tom Morris. It is rumoured that a sketch book exists that contains a number of drawings of this ghost. The book is said to have been owned by one of the managers of the residence who, after having had regular sightings of the figure reported to her, started to ask people to draw what they saw. Each time, over many years, the drawings were of the same man.

Other spectres are claimed to relate to student deaths within the building. The ghost of one is said to be seen walking down the central staircase and towards the main door, as though leaving, before vanishing. The story around this spook is that one of the students had fallen from his room window while watching for his parent's arrival, and he still walks down the stairs as though he is going to meet them. It is also rumoured that two students died in a fire on the top floor of the building, and they still haunt their old rooms. This story was, in part, fuelled by the fact there was indeed a fire in the building in 1976, when a painter working on the upper floor ignited part of the building while using a blow torch. Extensive damage was caused to the top floor and the roof, with one of the copper domes being destroyed and subsequently replaced with a fibre glass replica (as part of the renovation work carried out by the Kohler Company, this replica has now been replaced with a metal dome to exactly match the original). Following the fire, the access to the upper floor was sealed off and signs put up to warn students against trying to gain entry. This resulted in gossip that the restricted access was due to the student deaths and subsequent claims were made that the ghosts of these students haunt the upper floor causing a lot of paranormal activity, and these tales seem to have persisted through generations of students. There is however no record of any student deaths within the building, and the access to the top floor was sealed after the fire on the recommendation of the fire service, due to there being inadequate means of escape.

The most common reports in the building relate to heavy footsteps in the corridors. While it is easy to put this down to student high-jinx, some reports tell that the footsteps have been heard coming down the corridor towards a room at the end, where they stop. When looking out, the occupants of the room always finds there is no-one there and there is nowhere anyone could have gone other than back along the corridor. These type of disturbances have been reported as occurring for many years, and at different times of the year, including when there were few students in the building due to being outwith term time. Only time will tell whether these reports continue now that the building has started a new chapter in its life.

Hamilton Halls and Royal and Ancient viewed from the beach

WITCH LAKE AND WITCH HILL

Opposite the Hamilton Grand, on The Scores side, there is a grassy area that is a popular place for both locals and tourists to stop on a summer's day to take in the view out to sea. The needle shaped Martyrs' Monument also stands here, a poignant memorial to the protestant reformers who suffered terribly in the area during the reformation, and a band stand at the bottom of the steep slope is all that remains of a bygone day when the residents would come to stand on the then terraced grass embankment to listen to bands playing.

Band Stand with Witch Hill beyond

Looking further back in history however, the top end of this area was used for far more macabre uses. This was where many women, and some men, who had been accused of witchcraft faced their final judgement after the Witchcraft Act was introduced in Scotland in 1563, which made it punishable by death to either be a witch, or to consult a witch. The grass area was known as Witch Hill, and the water below known as the

Witch Lake. It was in the Witch Lake that the accused are said to have faced the process of 'ducking'. With their right thumb tied to their left toe, and their left thumb tied to their right toe, thereby forming the cross of St Andrew with their limbs across their body, these unfortunate people were thrown into the water at Witch Lake. If they drowned, they were innocent (but dead), and if they floated, this was considered evidence that they were being rejected by the purity of the water, and so must have the devil's mark. Those that floated were fished out, taken up to Witch Hill, and burned at the stake. Essentially, if you were accused of witchcraft at that time, it was very unlikely you would escape with your life. It was on Witch Hill that, on the 28th May 1588, a local woman named Alison Pearson lost her life in front of a crowd baying for blood.

Alison's story started with a ghostly encounter several decades before, when she was a young girl. She lived just a few miles outside St Andrews at Byrehills (now known as Boarhills), but she was a poorly child, with some reports indicating she had been born with a crippling illness. One of Alison's duties as a child was to collect herbs and plants for her family's use, and it was while doing so when she was around twelve years old at a den close to the village of Dunino that Alison fell desperately ill. As she lay on the hillside, clinging onto life, a familiar figure is said to have appeared to her, it was her cousin on her mother's side, William Simpson. William had in fact died several years earlier and, although recognisable as her cousin, he appeared in the form of a green man, a well-known pagan deity, normally depicted with foliage around his face, who is said to represent the spirits of the trees and plants as well as rebirth. He spoke to Alison and told her that if she confirmed her belief in him, he would help her and cure her of her illness. In her weakened state, Alison stated, without fear or hesitation, that she did believe in her cousin. William disappeared but soon returned along with a group that she recognised as faeries. Unlike the modern 'fairies', made popular in children's books and cartoons, faeries in history were unkind and mischievous characters. Often described as being spirits that were too bad to enter Heaven but too good to enter Hell, they were trapped with the living, and were certainly not a group that you would wish to upset, as their revenge could be brutal. One account of faerie vengeance, retold in the 1976 book *'Strange Tales of Bygone Fife'*, describes how a crime (possibly a murder) was committed in a house at Inchdairnie, a small, now gone, settlement close to the new town of Glenrothes in Fife. This crime in some way offended the faeries and resulted in them tearing down the house one night. The owners tried to rebuild the house but every time they reached a certain height, it was again torn down by the faeries until, eventually, all hopes of restoring the house were abandoned. In Alison's tale, the faeries are said to have taken her to Elfhame, a legendary hidden faerie land often referred to in the folklore of the lowlands of Scotland and the north of England. She was introduced to the Queen of Elfhame before, under the supervision of her cousin, she began to be trained by the faeries in the art of herbal remedies that could 'kill or cure, as desired'. Alison herself, made a full recovery from her illness and returned to live with her family, though for many years she was transported back to Elfhame for periods of time to continue her training. Initially she was treated badly by the faeries, who would beat her, but over time she gained their trust through her willingness to learn and she became proficient at creating their remedies.

In Fife, Alison's reputation grew and she became recognised and respected as a 'wise woman' that the locals would go to for cures for their various illnesses or injuries. As her fame spread, she came to the attention of the authorities, which would have fatal consequences for her. In 1583, she was called upon to tend to Patrick Hamilton, the archbishop of St Andrews, who was suffering from what is described as a 'serious illness'. Alison successfully cured the archbishop at a house in South Street and, legend has it, transferred his illness to a white horse that subsequently died. This was enough for Hamilton's many enemies to make accusations of witchcraft against Alison. If they could prove Alison was a witch and that she aided Hamilton, he too would be found guilty under the Witchcraft act of 1563 due to his consultation with a witch, and he too would be sentenced to death. A few months later, Alison was arrested and imprisoned under the charge of witchcraft, a charge that few ever managed to escape with their life.

During her trial, which no doubt involved considerable torture, Alison confessed to her involvement with the faeries and the Queen of Elfhame and was found guilty of being a witch. During the trial, Hamilton was left in the difficult position where he knew that speaking up to defend the woman who had cured him and potentially saved his life, would ultimately lead him to his own death. He considered that Alison's fate had been sealed when she was first accused and he knew that she would have little chance of being found innocent, and so he chose to remain quiet and save himself, thus denying his opponents of the evidence of his consultation with a witch that they needed.

In a bizarre twist, once convicted, Alison was handed over to Archbishop Hamilton to be detained in St Andrews castle until her execution. While she was held there, Alison miraculously managed to escape, avoiding the guards and overcoming the castles defensive walls and moat. There can be little doubt that her escape was aided by Archbishop Hamilton, who was finally able to show her his gratitude for her cures.

Alison avoided detection for a further five years until, in 1588, she was captured and underwent a second trial for witchcraft, when she was again found guilty. Patrick Hamilton by this time was fighting accusations that had been made against him of heresy, that would ultimately result in him being excommunicated, and so he was unable to assist. Having been found guilty, Alison was sentenced to death and burned at the stake on Witch Hill, with the only mercy being that she was strangled to death first, no doubt due to her confession.

The area by witch hill, now known as Bow Butts, was previously known as Methven's Tower and was considered a dreaded place, which is perhaps why it was chosen to burn those accused of witchcraft. There is also an older link with the area, which connects it to the story of Alison Pearson. The hill was also known as Fairy Knowe, a hill believed to contain part of the faerie kingdom, and possibly where Alison was taken by her cousin to be trained in the art of herbal medicine. It seems ironic that, whether by coincidence or by fate, this would ultimately be the spot Alison lost her life. At the den close to where Alison is said to have had her first encounter with her cousin in the form of a green man, a number of ancient carvings remain in the wall and, although substantially weather worn, these include one that appears to be a green man. It has to be questioned whether this could possibly be the image of Alison's cousin, William Simpson.

Green Man Carving

The spirit of Alison Pearson has been associated with later witch trials, where her ghost was said to have lured women to Elfhame, just as her deceased cousin had done to her. There are also reports of the ghostly figure of a woman being seen in the area around witch hill, often looking over the cliffs to the sea below where Witch Lake was once situated. The woman is however described as being elderly and with witch like features, and so this is unlikely to be the ghost of Alison Pearson as she would have still been a relatively young woman when she died. In addition to the phantom witch, it is believed that there is another, far more menacing spectre that also lurks in this area where so many innocent men and women lost their lives.

Several people have reported being followed by this menacing figure while walking late at night in the area. One early report of an encounter with this wraith tells that while walking home along The Scores after a night out, a young man suddenly became aware that he was not alone. When looking back, he spotted a dark figure standing behind the gates leading to the Step Rock swimming baths (which were built at Witch Lake). He felt unnerved by the figure, no-one should have been at the swimming baths at that time of night, but he was not overly concerned as the person was behind the iron gates. He still quickened his pace and when he glanced back again a few seconds later, he saw the figure had passed through the locked gates and was moving towards him. He froze with fear and could only stand and watch as the black, figure like mass, with no identifiable features, approached him at an ever quickening pace. The next thing he recalled was lying on the pavement with a police officer tending to him. Once he was fully conscious, the police officer explained that he had also been on The Scores and had noticed the man acting strangely, before he passed out. The police officer had witnessed the whole incident, but had not seen the dark figure and, although only a matter of seconds had passed, there was no sign of anyone else in the area.

Another account of this story is told in the 1983 book, '*A Haunting of Ghosts*', by Helen Cook. In this account, it is said that the figure wore clothing that appeared to be clerical, of a similar style to those that would be worn a long time ago. There was however no sign of a cross anywhere on the clothing or about the figure, who is described as emanating evil and having a musty smell. The figure's clothing also appeared completely dry, despite it being a stormy night with heavy rain. In this version the witness did not pass out, but was found by the police officer standing at the roadside, staring blankly across towards the step rock and the sea beyond.

Whether the police officer's intervention prevented anything worse happening to the young man will never be known. When searching newspaper archives, there does seem to be a notably high number of unfortunate incidents in this particular area. In July 1849, the *Fife Herald* reported that a female resident of the town had died suddenly while walking in the vicinity of the Martyrs' Monument the evening before. She was described as being in good health but was suddenly 'seized with the spasms of the fell destroyer', a choice of words that implies something ominous. As with the earlier case described, the woman was tended to quickly, but in this instance unfortunately did not survive, with the report stating that within a few minutes 'she was a corpse'. The cause of death had not been determined at the time of reporting.

In December 1864, the *Dundee Courier* reported that the body of a local man had been found at the Step Rock. He had gone missing the night before and his death is described as being 'completely shrouded in mystery'. In February 1868, the *Fife Herald* reported that the body of a local man had been found at Witch Hill with a significant head injury. Attending medics discovered he had been dead for some time and the cause of the injury was not known. In July 1868, the same paper reported that a 'melancholy drowning' had taken place at the Step Rock the day before. It states that a local coachbuilder had gone for an early morning swim and, as he was not a particularly good swimmer, had stayed at the shallowest area where the water was only six to seven feet deep. Some local boys, who were also at the pool, warned him not to swim there (the reason is not given) but the man persisted and having 'made a few splashes' he 'sank'. Despite the best efforts of the boys and the relatively shallow water, they were unable to bring him back to the surface. A local man who had witnessed the incident from his garden rushed to help and managed to get the man ashore, but he was already dead.

In September 1873, the *Fife Herald* told of another tragic accident at the Step Rock. A young man from the nearby town of Cupar is reported to have visited St Andrews where he went to swim at the Step Rock. Having swum out some distance, his swimming companion turned back due to the sea swell, and so he also turned to swim for shore. Inexplicably, he stopped and turned to lie on his back, making no swimming motion, allowing the current to carry him further out to sea. When he was around another fifty feet from the cliffs of Witch Hill, he suddenly seemed to come to his senses and began to swim towards a rock known locally as 'the black rock', where he would have been able to wait for rescue. Despite three attempts, the waves drove him back from the rocks before he 'sank in the presence of many, never to rise again'. The 'many' referred to were the assembled onlookers who had been unable to offer assistance due to the worsening sea conditions. While the incident is tragic enough, it is perhaps made worse by the fact that among the onlookers were the young man's three brothers, who witnessed the devastating event from the top of the cliffs at Witch Hill.

The Cliffs above Witch Lake (part obstructed by new Sealife Centre Building)

In August 1878, the *Fife Herald* reported that a much respected twenty year old man had been swimming at Witch Lake, as he did most evenings. When he reached some lifesaving equipment installed by the Humane Society, he was seen to climb out of the water but suddenly fell back in. It is assumed he was gripped by something unseen, speculated to have been cramp. Despite efforts to rescue him, he drowned. In August 1897, the *Dundee Courier* reported that the son of a prominent Edinburgh family had been found dead in Witch Lake. He had been last seen leaving the Royal and Ancient golf club the night before just before midnight, walking towards his hotel by the shore, which would take him by the lake and Witch Hill. The only injury to his body was an abrasion to the side of his head.

I have deliberately avoided giving the names of any of those who perished out of respect to the families and it would off course be completely wrong to state that any of these cases are directly associated with the reported haunting in the area. While the cases of drowning could be explained simply by the sea current, St Andrews is fortunate enough to have many miles of beaches providing plenty of room for swimming, yet incidents in the other areas seem scarce in comparison. The reports I have given are just a few examples of the many terrible events that have occurred in this area, where so many are believed to have been previously drowned to prove their innocence and many more were burned to death, and I find it unusual that tragedy seems to continue here.

A number of skeletons have also been found in the area due to coastal erosion, although the claims by some that 'hundreds' have been found seem grossly exaggerated. In 1904, part of the cliff at Witch Lake collapsed following a major storm, revealing two skeletons. They were determined to be between four and five hundred years old and, due to the burial position, were deemed to have been given a Christian burial. This would exclude the possibility that the bodies were in any way connected to the witch trials as the remains of those convicted of witchcraft were denied a Christian burial. In 1906 another part of the cliff face collapsed revealing more bones, indicating that the site may have been an early burial site. Soon after this incident, the cliffs were strengthened to prevent further erosion and collapse, and so it is unknown how many bodies may still lie below the ground.

Who, or what, the dark figure that walks this area is will probably never be known. Personally, I feel 'what' is a more appropriate description for it and I relate that to a reputedly evil ghost that lurks within one of the rooms in the famous Edinburgh underground vaults. Often described as being a featureless, black figure, this spook is believed to be a poltergeist of not one spirit, but created by the spirits of many who all perished while trapped in the room during a fire. It seems particularly active with a dislike to women, so much so that on tours it is not uncommon for the men and women on a tour of the vaults to be separated for this room only, with the women told to stand on the side of the room where the poltergeist is less active. Is it possible that the hundreds of tortured souls who met their deaths at witch hill and in the waters below have similarly created a poltergeist? That is a question that I doubt I will ever be able to answer with definitive evidence, but it may offer a possible explanation.

Further examples of poltergeist activity occurred at a small tearoom named The Pavillion, which once stood perched at the side of the sea.

The Pavillion

As a child, The Pavillion was a regular stop for a cold drink or ice cream on hot summer days, and the lady who ran it used to tell me that she would often find the place in a state of some disarray when she opened up in the morning, with cans of juice and other items lying on the ground. At the time we wondered if this was due to the sea causing the building to shake during high tides, however, I have recently managed to contact this lady's son and daughter who were able to confirm that a number of strange occurrences happened, which also included coffee cups being found laid out on the tables when they had been put away the night before. This is clearly not something that could have happened as a result of vibrations in the building, but it is the type of activity associated with a poltergeist and the close proximity of The Pavillion to the Step Rock would suggest it was the same spirit at work.

Incidentally, I believe I may have been involved in an encounter with this phantom in my younger days. On an evening out, having enjoyed a few drinks with two friends at one of the bars along the Scores, we decided to move on. One of my friends left first, and by the time my other friend and I reached the street, there were no signs of him. Younger readers may not see this as a particular problem, but back then we did not have the luxury of things like mobile phones, so we did not know which direction he had went in and, as we had not already decided where we were going next, we did not want to leave without him. After a short search, we heard him calling from the bottom of the hill across the road at Bow Butts. We found him lying on the grass close to the gated entrance to the former Step Rock Swimming Baths, which by then had been converted into the Sealife Centre. He explained that when he left the bar, he had seen a figure standing close to the Martyrs' Monument. He felt he knew the person and the urge to go over to see him but, when he did so he had lost his footing and had fallen down the hill, to where we found him. There was no sign of anyone else around and we put it down to him having one too many drinks and wanting to relive his youth by rolling down the hill. After having a laugh about it, we headed to the next bar, but had I known then what I know now about the area, I may not have been quite so quick to dismiss it.

Witch Hill and the Martyrs' Monument

THE SMOTHERED PIPER'S CAVE

Further along The Scores, somewhere in the cliffs below the Principal's House of St Andrews University, lies the hidden entrance to a cave that has caused much mystery in St Andrews for centuries.

The Principal's House

The entrance to the cave, which was in an elevated position above the high tide line, could only be accessed by climbing the rocks at the base of the cliff at low tide. Although many knew of the cave, few approached its entrance and even fewer dared to venture into its murky depths, due to it being believed to be a place of evil and terror. Those who did brave the darkness, were able to provide a description of the interior of the cave. From the information given, it seems the narrow, triangular entrance did not truly indicate what lay beyond the tunnel on the other side. Although having to stoop to enter, the tunnel soon enlarged allowing a man to stand at full height. The tunnel sloped down steeply for around fifty feet, before levelling and continuing for another seventy feet. At this point, it is said to have descended into a large chamber, at the back of which the entrances to two further passageways lay. Carved into the rock, between these two entrances, was a cross, indicating that the cavern may have had earlier religious uses. It seems no-one had dared venture beyond this point, or if they had, they didn't speak of what they had encountered.

There had always been much speculation about these tunnels, and where they led, and local legend has it that on New Year's Eve many years ago, a young piper named Jock (predictably!) took up a bet to venture into the cave and tunnels beyond to see what he could find. It was agreed that he would play his pipes as he walked, in the hope that this would allow people on the surface to follow his progress, showing above ground where the tunnels led. His wife begged him not to go, but Jock was determined to solve the mystery of this cave, once and for all.

In front of a small crowd of people and his pleading wife, Jock climbed up and entered the cave, before beginning to play his pipes. Others watched from above, peering over the cliff edge, and then excitedly moving away, following the sound of the pipes as Jock ventured further into the tunnels. The route that the sound of the pipes took is not noted, although some reports say they were heard as far as Market Street, before they suddenly stopped, never to be heard again.

Jock's distraught wife waited at the cave entrance for days hoping he would return, but he never did. Despite some locals entering the cave in an attempt to find him, it seemed no-one had the courage to go very far into the darkness. Young Jock was lost.

A year later, again on Hogmanay, the tale tells that Jock's wife left her house, reputedly telling people that she was 'going to her Jock'. She ventured down to the foot of the cliffs and to the cave entrance, and she too was never seen again. Whether she went into the caves seeking her husband, or whether she slipped and was washed out to sea, would never be known.

Since Jock went missing, it is reported that his ghost has been seen many times walking along an area of the West Cliffs where it would be physically impossible for anyone to now walk due to the coastal erosion. His pipes have also been heard, but this is something that no-one wishes to hear, as they are considered to be a warning that a death will occur within a year. The spirit of Jock's wife has also been reported, either kneeling or pacing back and forwards in front of the cave entrance, forever waiting for her husband to return.

The entrance to the cave was unfortunately covered a long time ago, due partly to the cliff face collapsing and also due to building work to construct houses along the top of the cliffs and the tunnel was believed to have been lost until, on 24th June 1946, the *Dundee Courier* reported that it may have been found once again. The article, headed 'Haunt of Ghostly Piper', covers the legend of the piper and goes on to tell that during alteration work at the James Mackenzie Clinical Institute (now the Scores Hotel), workmen had accidentally uncovered a tunnel in the basement cellar at the front of the building.

The Scores Hotel

The passageway travelled north towards the sea, and was partly cut from the rock and partly made up from built up stones. A short distance along the tunnel, it had collapsed and was blocked, and so an application for a permit to unblock the passageway was to be submitted to the local authority by Captain Douglas Percival, who was overseeing the work. The workmen also believed that the basement had cut into the tunnel, and that it would have continued again from the opposite side of the building.

I have tried to find out from Fife Councils archives whether such an application was ever made and, if so, what was found, but unfortunately there are no records held. With nothing else said in the town about the discovery of the passageway, it seems that either it was found to be something else or, as was frequently the case, no exploration was made to prevent any delays in the work on the building.

My grandfather used to tell me that as a child he had found a cave entrance at the cliffs that he believed was the piper's cave before the entrance had collapsed, and he had ventured in. He only got a short distance before further progress was prevented by a metal gate, which had led him to believe that the access to the cavern and the passageways beyond had been blocked to prevent people from wandering in. Enquiries with the archaeologists at Fife Council suggest that others have also entered the same cave and encountered the gate, though they managed to see what appeared to be machinery on the other side. From the details given, it would seem this is more likely to have been a cave known as the Smugglers Cave, and the machinery may have been the pumps for a public swimming pool that once stood on the cliff top above. It therefore seems that the location of young Jock's cave will remain a mystery, although there has been a belief for a long time that there is a network of underground passageways below old St Andrews and so it is possible that they will one day be found and accessed, revealing their secrets.

In another take relating to the Principal's House, I was given a personal account of a haunting while carrying out the research for this book by a lady named Iona. She informed me that in the early part of the twentieth century, her mother worked as a nanny for, as far as she could recall, the Haig family, while they lived on the Scores, although she was not sure which property it was. Field Marshall Sir Douglas Haig was the rector of St Andrews University from 1916 to 1919, which leads me to believe this incident may have occurred in the Principal's House.

Iona told me that her mother used to recall that while working for the family, she witnessed a veiled lady coming down the stairs. The sight of the figure must have terrified her as she fainted. When she came round, she told a family member what she had seen and was rather unsympathetically told that this meant she would either become seriously ill or die within six months! Sure enough, around six months later, she was fighting for her life with pneumonia in the town's cottage hospital. Fortunately, she won the battle and lived to tell the tale.

The family's reaction to the sighting would indicate they were familiar with this spirit and the consequences of her appearance, implying the ghost may be connected to the family, but no more information is available.

While walking along the Scores, I would encourage anyone to take their eyes from the sea view for a while and take in the splendour of the houses on the opposite side of the road, not just for their architectural interest, but to also contemplate how many spirits still dwell here, connected the families who once occupied them.

CASTLECLIFFE, THE SCORES

Continuing along the Scores, just before the castle, a large stone mansion sits on the cliff side. Known as Castlecliffe, this category B listed building was constructed in 1869 in Scots Baronial style for a prominent chemist at the university, Professor Thomas Purdie, after whom the School of Chemistry is now named.

Castlecliffe

Among the unusual features that Castlecliffe can claim are a secret door disguised as a book case, which was designed to be used by the servants, and a staircase carved into the cliffs leading to a natural rock swimming pool. During World War One, the building was used as an auxiliary hospital, after which St Leonards private school took ownership and it was used as dormitories. The building was later sold to St Andrews University, and initially used as the Spanish department before becoming the School of Economics, as it is still used today.

It was while it was in use as the Spanish Department, that a report of a ghostly sighting of a soldier was made at Castlecliffe. A student is said to have been making their way to the office of the Head of School, when he noticed a man waiting patiently at the door. The man appeared to be dressed in a uniform from WW1 and, as the student approached, he simply disappeared. No one else had seen a soldier anywhere in the building that day, but he has been seen several times since. According to the November 2009 edition of the St Andrews University staff magazine, the *StAndard*, the strange sightings were mentioned many years later by one of the grounds men at the Castle to some of the staff at Castlecliffe, and they were able to come up with a possible explanation for the appearance of the soldier. They told the magazine that a soldier had indeed died at Castlecliffe, in somewhat tragic circumstances. He had returned to St Andrews from the war and, due to him being awarded the Victoria Cross, the highest military decoration awarded for courage in the face of the enemy, he became a local celebrity. The soldier had continued to work around the town, but unable to deal with the pressure his status had brought, he had turned to alcohol and while cleaning the windows at Castlecliffe, he fell off the ladder and died.

The magazine carried out some research and found that there was a soldier who fitted the description given, Corporal John Ripley of the first battalion of the Black Watch who had won the Victoria Cross for his bravery at the Battle of Aubers in France on 9th May 1915, after which he was promoted to sergeant. When the war ended, he returned to St Andrews, where he died in 1933.

Keen to seek some more details, I searched the newspaper archives and found a report in the *Dundee Evening Telegraph* from 15th July 1915 that states that a 'hero's welcome' had been organised for Sergeant Ripley, V.C., with a crowd of several hundred people gathered at the station, along with the pipe band of the 7th Black Watch. However, he did not appear, with the paper speculating that he was too modest to face the crowds, which further matches the details provided of the soldier who died at Castlecliffe. The Black Watch Castle and Museum website provides details of Sergeant Ripley's actions leading to the award of the Victoria Cross stating:

When leading his section on the right of the right platoon in the assault he was the first man of the Battalion to ascend the enemy's parapet and from there he directed those following him to the gaps in the German wire entanglements, he then led his Section through a break in the parapet to a second line of trench which had previously been decided upon as the final objective in this part of the line. In that position Cpl Ripley with 7 or 8 men established himself, blocking both flanks and arranging a fire position until all his men had fallen and he himself had been badly wounded in the head.'

Sergeant Ripley, V.C. (Photo supplied by Black Watch Museum)

In the *Dundee Courier*, dated August 15th 1933, details of his death are given which confirm the location. It is stated that he had been employed as a slater (rather than a window cleaner) and, while working at Castlecliffe, he had fallen eighteen feet from his ladder suffering severe spinal injuries. He died later that day in the town's Cottage Hospital at the age of sixty six. Given his age and that Sergeant Ripley had suffered head injuries in war, it would appear this is the most likely reason for his fall, rather than the perhaps unjust inference that alcohol was involved.

Rear view of Castlecliffe

ST ANDREWS CASTLE

At the top of the Scores, St Andrews castle comes into full view. This impressive ruin sits on a rocky outcrop in a commanding position overlooking St Andrews bay and to the North Sea beyond.

St Andrews Castle

In the tenth century, the bishops of St Andrews gained control of the Scottish church and, following the commencement of work on St Andrews cathedral in the twelfth century, Bishop Roger (1189-1202) instructed the castle to be built to provide a defensive residence for himself, and successive bishops and later archbishops. The building was extensively damaged during the Wars of Independence with England, which were fought from 1296 to 1328, and 1332 to 1357. In 1385, the castle was repaired and restored on the order of Bishop Walter Trail and, over the following decades, additional defences were added to deal with the rising religious tension, particularly due to the Scottish Reformation, a religious conflict between Protestants and Catholics. The castle again suffered considerable damage during a siege to end a short period of Protestant occupation, which will be discussed in more detail later.

Rebuilding work followed, including a new frontage, however in 1592, the Golden Act as it is now known, returned the Presbyterian influence on the church and ended the need for a bishop, or their residence, leading to the castle being abandoned and quickly falling into a state of disrepair. In 1801 the great hall was lost to the sea, and the cliff erosion continued until a sea wall was constructed to protect the ruins in 1886.

With such a long history, and the castles residents role in various religious battles, it is not surprising to learn that there are several tales of ghostly goings-on within and around its walls, the most well-known of which is probably Cardinal David Beaton, the Archbishop of St Andrews from 1539 to 1546. Beaton had already won the trust of King James V through his role in arranging the marriage between the king and Madeleine (the daughter of King Francois I of France) in 1537. Madeleine died shortly after, and Beaton again assisted in arranging the King's marriage to his second wife, Marie de Guise, in 1538. Influenced by Beaton's ties with the French, King James started to move his alliance, and that of Scotland, to France and away from King Henry VIII of England. When King James died in 1542, leaving his six day old daughter Mary, Queen of Scots, as the heir to the throne, Beaton wasted no time in trying to gain the role of regent to the infant queen, which would allow him to have significant influence in the control of the country. Scotland at this time was thrown into turmoil. Religious unsettlement had already started, and both King Henry VIII of England and King Henri II of France sought to gain control of the Scottish Crown through marriage.

If Henry's son, Edward (also still an infant) was to marry Queen Mary, this would give Protestant England control over the mainly Catholic Scotland, whereas if Henri's son, Francis, was to marry the queen, this would re-enforce the connection between Scotland and France, which was also a Catholic country, and would form a formidable threat to England, both in military and religious terms.

A period known as 'the rough wooing' started when King Henry of England commenced offensive raids into Scotland, in an attempt to force the Scottish people to agree to the marriage of Edward and Mary, while the French provided the Scots with the necessary firepower to stop the advancing English army. Both countries are said to have spent a fortune in their attempts to gain the hand of Queen Mary. Ultimately, it was the French who were successful and, in 1548, five year old Mary sailed to France to be raised in the French Court, alongside Francis.

During this time, Cardinal Beaton had started a brutal personal battle against the Protestants and, declaring them as heretics, he began rounding them up to be executed. Many Scots believed it was Beaton's actions that had led King Henry of England to commence the 'rough wooing' tactics, resulting in considerable loss of life and Beaton becoming an increasingly unpopular character, with rumours that he was in league with the Devil. In 1546 he made his final error, when he had a popular Protestant preacher named George Wishart arrested. After a sham trial, Wishart was burned at the stake outside St Andrews Castle on 1st March 1546.

It is probably worthwhile adding some detail about this method of execution, as it tends to generate various images. In a larger fire, such as those where several people were burned at the same time, experts consider that the victims would have died, or at least passed out, due to smoke inhalation before the flames actually reach them. In a smaller, single person fire, the victim would suffer extensive burns before either succumbing to the pain or the smoke inhalation. In Scotland it was common to choke the condemned to death at the stake prior to the fire being lit rather than burning them alive. This was also a horrific death, with the most common method being a loop of rope passing through a hole in the stake, around the neck, and then back through the hole. Either end of the rope was then attached to a piece of wood, which was slowly turned to tighten the rope, pulling the head of the victim back against the stake, before starting to choke them. Once sufficient pressure was achieved to make breathing either very difficult or impossible, the tension in the rope would be held until the victim was dead.

In the case of George Wishart a small fire was used and he was to be burned alive, no doubt to send out a warning to other Protestant Reformers of the fate that awaited them if caught. As if this method of execution wasn't bad enough, the well-intended actions of a supporter may have added to Wishart's agony. It is said a small bag of gunpowder was placed in the fire with the intention that when it detonated it would kill Wishart, saving him from the flames. Unfortunately, the explosion was of insufficient strength and only succeeded in causing significant injuries to one side of Wishart and reducing the ferocity of the fire for a while, prolonging his excruciating death. Beaton is reported to have watched the entire burning from the luxury of his castle, an action that did not go unnoticed by his enemies.

Wishart's popularity would ultimately be Beaton's downfall. A plot was started against him and on 29th May, 1546, a group of ten men silently joined the workmen (who ironically had been appointed to strengthen the castle's defences) as they entered the castle in the morning. Splitting into two groups to reduce the risk of detection, the first group successfully made it past the guards, but the second group caught the attention of the gate porter who tried to raise the alarm. Those already inside swiftly grabbed him, took his keys and threw him into the moat. The workmen who witnessed this turned and fled, fearing for their lives, and this alerted Beaton to the attack. He secured himself in his chamber and initially refused to open the door, until his assailants threatened to burn it down. When they entered, they began what became a frenzied attack on Beaton, stabbing him multiple times and mutilating his body, which was then hung by an arm and a leg, so he formed the cross of St Andrew, from the window from which he had watched George Wishart burn.

The ghost of Beaton has been witnessed several times and in different locations. The bulk of the reports are that he is seen standing looking out of the window where he had been hung. The possibility of this figure being a visitor to the castle can easily be ruled out on the basis there is no floor at this level. His spirit has also been seen walking within the grounds of the castle and also in the sea tower, gazing across the bay towards Dundee. Interestingly, Claypotts Castle, which sits in an elevated position on the outskirts of Dundee, is said to be haunted by Marion Ogilvy, who was the mistress of Cardinal Beaton. Marion's ghost is reported to stand in one of the windows looking out towards St Andrews, with a sad expression and waving a handkerchief. The date she appears is 29th May, the day Cardinal Beaton was murdered. Could it be that the two lovers still gaze across to each other on the anniversary of Beaton's death?

The tale of Cardinal Beaton's ghost is well known within the town, and even in my youth people would happily tell the story, but when asked, few will tell you they have actually seen the phantom. Most have either heard it as it was passed down through families or 'know someone' who told them they saw the figure. Most will tell you that the ghost is seen at a large window at the front of the castle, but this is actually part of a defensive wall that was not built until after Beaton's death. Frustratingly, there are very few actual documented cases and most of the written accounts that do exist tend to come from students, always seeming to start with words along the line of 'we were returning from a drunken night out when…'. I lived in St Andrews long enough to know the level of intoxication that statement means, so I can state that I would not consider such reports as verified sightings!

Other ghosts associated with the castle are Archbishop Hamilton, the last Archbishop of St Andrews who, after being accused of the assassination of James Stewart, the Earl of Moray, was hung in Stirling. Although the shot that killed Stewart was fired from the Archbishop's residence in Linlithgow, it was actually his nephew who had fired it. The connection was however enough for his opponents to arrange the trial and execution, thus removing the position of Archbishop. Although Hamilton never stayed at St Andrews and did not die there, his ghost is said to have been witnessed in the grounds, still with the hangman's noose around his neck. It has also been claimed that the phantom of a woman in ancient clothing walks the castle grounds, passing through the barrier at the cliff edge and continuing to walk where parts of the castle fell into the sea a long time ago, before vanishing. As with Cardinal Beaton, documented sighting of these ghouls are also sadly lacking.

One of the most interesting features of the castle, believed to be the only one of its type in the world, was created in the time immediately after Cardinal Beaton's murder. His assailants secured themselves in the castle, confident that all they had to do was fend off the attacks from the local forces and wait until the English army arrived. Having removed Beaton from power, one of the main obstacles in King Henry's way, they were sure they would be rescued by his army. They did successfully hold the castle for a year, during which time there was an attempt to dig a tunnel into the castle to seize it. The mine, as it is known, started just beyond the spot where George Wishart was executed, and travels down below the moat and towards the castle. Aware of the ploy, those inside the castle also began to dig a tunnel, known as the counter-mine, with the intention to intercept the mine. After several false starts, the counter mine did miraculously meet the mine. Although the counter mine was at a higher level, as it passed over the mine its roof top collapsed, joining the two tunnels and no doubt catching anyone in the mine by surprise. Details of what happened after this are somewhat scarce, there seems little doubt there would have been a battle in the confined space to ultimately defeat the siege on the castle. Surprisingly, there are no ghost stories associated with this part of the castle, though in my personal opinion, if any part should be haunted it is the mine and counter-mine, which can still be accessed today.

The Mine Tunnel

Unfortunately for the Protestant Reformers inside the castle, it was the Catholic French forces that arrived before the English, and they bombarded the castle from the sea and the cathedral. The defences soon fell and those inside were taken prisoner, with some being put into slavery to serve in the French King's galleys. Among those sent to the galleys was a man named John Knox, probably the most famous of the Scottish reformers.

Knox was born a few miles outside Edinburgh. His exact date of birth is not known and ranges in documents from 1505 to 1514. He studied theology at St Andrews University and became ordained into priesthood prior to 1540. As mentioned earlier, Scotland by this time was going through religious turmoil with growing resentment against the Catholic Church, which had become a major landowner with significant wealth but with leaders who were seen as little more than political figures and who, like Cardinal Beaton, showed complete disregard for the Christian faith in the way they conducted themselves. Knox became influenced by the preaching of the early protestant reformers who were bringing the work of Martin Luther, a German theologian, across to Scotland from mainland Europe and by 1545, John Knox had openly declared his conversion to the Protestant faith. George Wishart had been a major influence in his life and Knox had taken the role of Wishart's bodyguard, travelling with him across the country. After Wishart's brutal death at the hands of Cardinal Beaton and the resultant occupation of St Andrews Castle by protestant reformers, John Knox was smuggled into the castle to continue teaching them the protestant faith. Although he had nothing to do with Cardinal Beaton's murder, when the castle was finally taken he was treated the same as those responsible, and spent eighteen months as a slave on the French galleys.

Upon his release, Knox returned to England where he was appointed as a preacher, initially in Berwick and then in London, where he continued his attacks on the Catholic faith. In 1553, Mary 1st became Queen of England and, fearful for his safety under the new Roman Catholic queen, Knox travelled to Europe where he remained until 1559. He then returned to Scotland where he became minister at St Andrews and then St Giles in Edinburgh, and continued to preach until his death in 1572.

In the 1983 book, *'A Haunting of Ghosts'*, by Helen Cook, a tale relating to the ghost of John Knox is recalled. It tells that in the early 1960s, a lady named Priscilla Robertson had been walking with her then fiancé, now husband, close to the castle late one spring evening when they spotted a young man standing staring at the castle. She described him as being well dressed, wearing a long cloak like garment and a skull cap, and he had a short pointed beard. He is said to have been completely absorbed watching the castle. When her fiancé turned on the torch he was carrying to aid their walk, they could no longer see the figure.

Neither felt scared by the experience and neither identified the man as John Knox. It was not until sometime later when Mrs Robertson was reading an illustrated biography of Knox that she saw a picture portraying him as a young man and she recognised him as the figure they had seen that night.

John Knox portrait, dated 24th December 1572

From the description given, it seems likely that the ghost of Knox was standing in the area where George Wishart, the man who had been so influential in his early life, was burned at the stake. This spot is marked with the letters 'GW' set into the road.

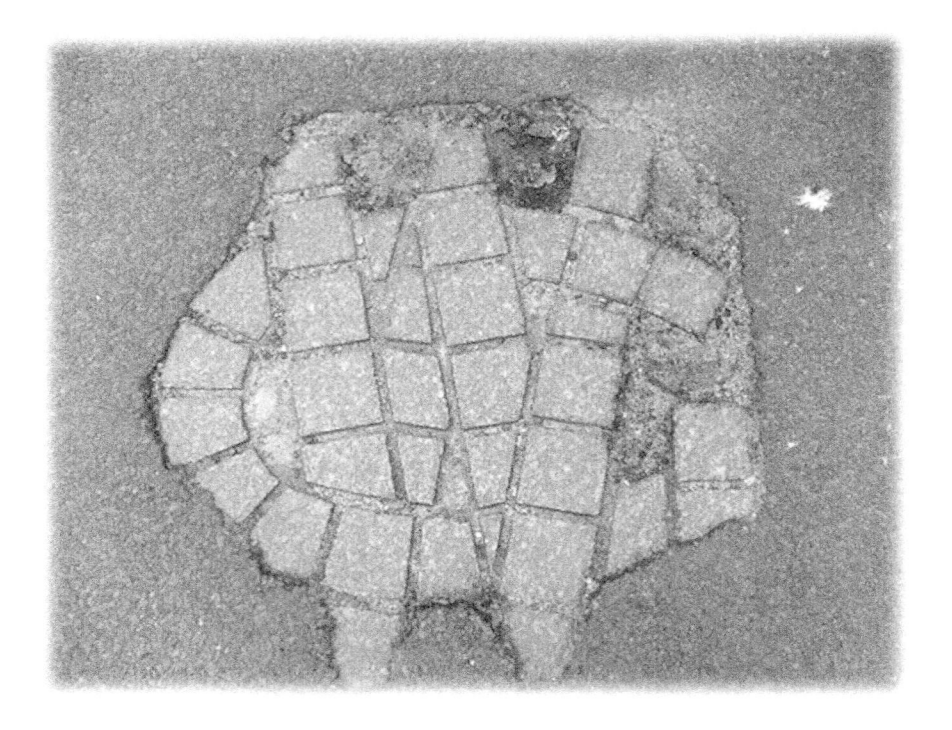

The spot where George Wishart was Burned to Death

LADY BUCHANAN'S CAVE

Just beyond the sands of the Castle Beach, a cave in the cliff side has a ghostly reputation. Commonly known as Lady Buchanan's cave, this natural rock chamber was originally relatively shallow, however, that was all to change in 1760 with the arrival in St Andrews of Henry David Erskine, the 10th Earl of Buchanan. Lord Buchanan had moved his family to St Andrews to aid the education of his son, Thomas Erskine, who would later go on to become the Lord Chancellor of the United Kingdom. Lord Buchanan's wife, Agnes Stuart, was considered to be self-motivated and ambitious, with a somewhat eccentric side. During their time in St Andrews, she chose this cave for an unusual place of entertainment. On her instructions, it was widened and deepened to form two chambers, with a door between them. The entrance sat above the sea line and a staircase was carved into the rock face along with a pathway to allow easier access to her grotto, which was then intricately decorated with sea shells. Lady Buchanan used the cave both as a place of solitude and as a place to hold tea parties with her friends right up to her death in 1778. Unfortunately the cave collapsed some time towards the end of the nineteenth century, and the staircase and pathway carved into the rocks were lost to the harsh coastal elements shortly after.

The Cliff Face where Lady Buchanan's Cave was situated

This was not believed to have been the first use of the cave, with reference to it being previously known as St Rule's Cave. St Rule was a Greek monk who brought the remains of Saint Andrew to Scotland in the early part of the first century. According to the legend, he was shipwrecked in what is now known as St Andrews Bay, and many versions of his story have him seeking shelter in a cave below where the first monastery would later be built. The cave at that time would have been quite different from the shallow depression Lady Buchanan had modified to her specification, as the cliff face had suffered extensive corrosion over the centuries and had been quarried. Assuming they were the same cave, it would therefore seem that the section used by Lady Buchanan was the remaining rear part of the original cave.

It is into the mouth of this earlier cave, described as a 'sea cave' indicating that the entrance to the original cave lay lower than that of Lady Buchanan's cave, that it is said a phantom ship has been witnessed sailing. Why a ship would sail into the cave, or even when these sightings were, remains a mystery, though that has not stopped the phantom ship becoming part of the local ghost-lore. There are also claims that the ghost of a pig is seen running from the cave and tumbling into the sea.

This seems to be another story passed down rather than documented, however it is worth bearing in mind that at the time of St Rule's arrival in Scotland, this area was over-run with wild pigs. The reader may have noticed that the St Andrews coat of arms, as shown at the start of the book, includes a boar to mark this connection.

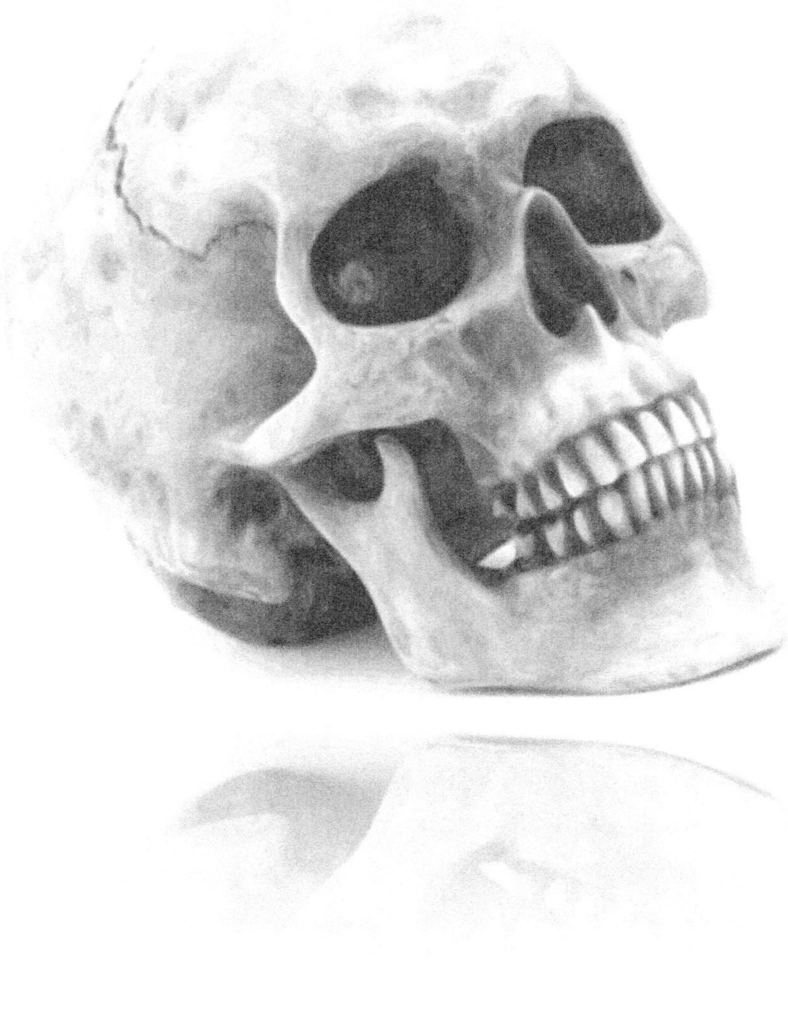

THE CATHEDRAL, THE PENDS AND THE HARBOUR

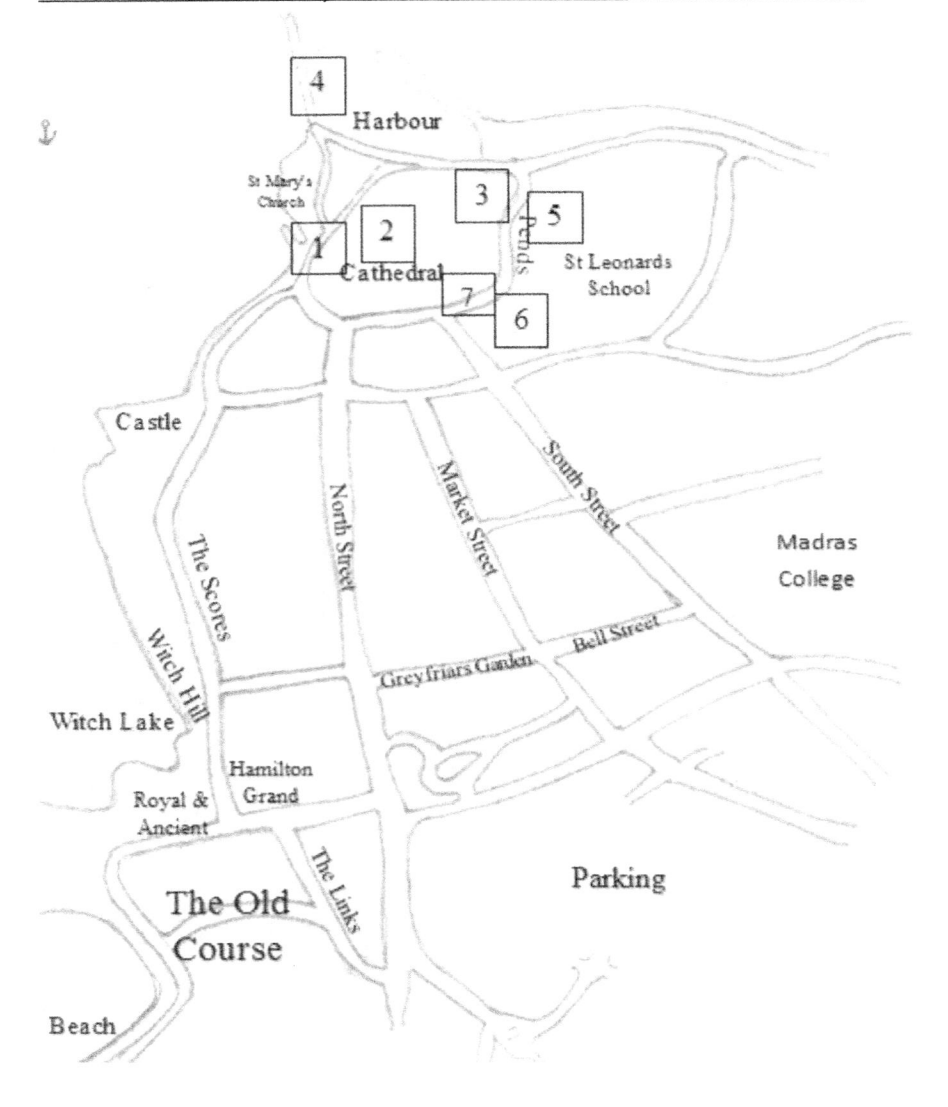

1) The Haunted Tower
2) St Rules Tower
3) The Eastern Cemetery
4) The Pier
5) The New Inns
6) The Nuns Walk
7) The Pends Archway

THE CATHEDRAL

On the eastern edge of St Andrews sits the cathedral, without a doubt one of the most impressive sights in the town, the ruins of which must be explored to fully appreciate the scale and the grandeur of the site. The remains can be somewhat confusing as they comprise of not just one, but two churches.

St Andrews Cathedral

The oldest building within the Cathedral grounds is St Rule's (or St Regulus) Tower, which is more commonly referred to as the 'Square Tower', due to its distinctive square shape. This is all that remains of St Rule's church, which was built around 1130, and provided an initial home for the priests, who were increasing in numbers due to the towns growing religious importance. By 1160, St Rule's church became too small and work on the main cathedral began to create better facilities. It took one hundred and fifty years to complete, with it being dedicated in the presence of King Robert the First (better known now as Robert the Bruce), in July 1318. Constructed in a traditional cruciform shape, and measuring three hundred and ninety one feet long (approximately one hundred and twenty metres) and one hundred and sixty eight feet wide (approximately fifty two metres), it was by far the largest church in Scotland and remains the largest ever built in the country.

View through the former ceremonial entrance with the rear tower in the distance

The surrounding ground was designated to be used as a cemetery and a tall defensive wall with watch towers enclosed the site, the remains of which are, according to Historic Scotland, the 'most complete and imposing monastic enclosure walls in Scotland'. The cathedral remained the headquarters of the medieval Scottish Church until the times of the reformation when, in June 1559, the Protestant Reformer John Knox delivered a particularly poignant and fierce sermon at the town's parish Church, after which the townsfolk immediately began to ransack the Cathedral. The attacks continued and it was finally abandoned, most likely through force, in 1561 and despite later plans for the restoration of the church, this never happened and the buildings were extensively quarried for stone to build the houses and shops that now occupy much of the town centre.

The best known ghost story from St Andrews is the White Lady, who is said to walk through the grounds of the cathedral. Reports of sightings describing a tall, beautiful woman, wearing a long white dress and white elbow length gloves, gliding silently towards one of the towers in the cathedral wall, before disappearing, have been made for centuries. The tower became to be treated with a mixture of suspicion and fear by the townsfolk, so much so that it became known as the Haunted Tower and few would dare pass it after dark.

The Haunted Tower

An unusual discovery, widely reported as occurring in 1868, shed some light on the mysterious phantom. After the centuries of desolation and neglect, the importance of sites such as the cathedral were once again being recognised for their historical significance and as potential tourist attractions. The initial stages of preparing the cathedral site involved clearing the years of dereliction and amassed rubbish, which resulted in the ground levels being lowered by around two to three feet (up to one metre). Stonemasons were assigned to carry out repairs to the newly exposed sections of walls throughout the site and those working on the tower, either by accident or deliberately, ended up removing some stones from the lowest part of the wall. Expecting to find a simple continuation of the stair to the original ground level, they were surprised to discover an entire lower chamber of the tower. It was not however the chamber that shocked them, it was what they found inside. The actual contents vary in different reports, although one thing remained consistent, there were bodies within the vault, one of which was finely dressed in white.

On 1st February 1894, the *Evening Telegraph* published a special report on the tower in an attempt to establish the facts. The article repeats an earlier report that the opening formed in the wall was just big enough for a man to crawl through. One of the masons did so, and continued to squeeze into the chamber until just his feet remained outside. His colleagues had been holding him and became aware that he had suddenly stopped moving, so they pulled him out only to discover he had fainted. Another of the men immediately crawled into the hole and he too had to be pulled out and, according to the article, was found to be 'in a very ill way'. A Professor of the United College was called and, unlike the other men, he managed to fully enter the chamber. A short while later, he emerged, with the body of a woman in his arms. From the descriptions given, the corpse was very well preserved, appearing as though it had only just been buried, which would have been impossible. The professor advised there were a total of twelve corpses in the tomb, all showing almost no sign of decay, and so advice was sought from the Lord-Advocate. The instructions given were to return the body and re-seal the chamber, and nothing more was to be said about it!

The reporter spoke to Mr Jesse Hall who, a Gas Manager and representative of the Woods and Forest Department, was involved in overseeing the work at the cathedral. He came across as quite dismissive initially in his responses, apparently unwilling to enter into the subsequent speculation about the discoveries. He did confirm that as part of the reduction of the ground level, a lower chamber was uncovered at the tower. This was full of bones, but it was found that a sexton (a church officer responsible for the maintenance of the church buildings and graveyard) had been 'disposing' of bones by putting them through a small opening in the tower. He also confirmed that while a stonemason was carrying out some pointing work on the tower, one of the stones was knocked out. When looking inside, it could be seen that there were a few steps leading to a doorway that had been blocked up with stone. At this stage, the stories seem to be getting confused. The initial reports implied that the stonemasons accessed the burial chamber, whereas based on the statement from Mr Hall, they could have only accessed a vault containing the stairs. They would have had to enter this and remove stones from the blocked up door to gain access to the chamber.

Mr Hall then provided the reporter with notes taken by a Mr Smith, a watchmaker in the town who was present at the opening of the vault and wrote down his account of what happened. He recorded that for some time he had tried to gain permission to access the sealed chamber and on 7th September 1868, accompanied by three colleagues, they made a hole in the blocked up doorway, just large enough for them to slide through. By this time he noted the lower vault had been cleared, presumably referring to the bones that had been put there by the sexton. Once inside the chamber, they found approximately ten coffins piled on top of each other, each containing well preserved bodies, one of which was a female wearing long white leather gloves. He stated there was a monument stone within the chamber but it was so badly worn it was impossible to make out any of the writing, and so the identity of the bodies remained a mystery. It seems the chamber was then sealed again, with the suggestion that one of the stonemasons took one of the gloves, a suggestion that Mr Hall did not appear to believe.

Mr Smith was later keen to access the chamber again and Mr Hall confirmed he received a number of requests, but that he 'did not care about it' and 'did not like to disturb the dead'. He did however relent and, accompanied by Mr Smith and Mr Walker, the university librarian, they proceeded to again make a small hole in the wall to the chamber.

They did so in the early hours of the morning to avoid attracting attention as they knew the tower still generated a lot of local interest. Mr Hall states that on this occasion, the three men again found the coffins, of which he estimated there was around six, with two lying on the ground, and the rest piled on top of each other. Only one coffin was found to contain a body, which he described as a girl, approximately four and a half feet tall, and with a mummified appearance. She was naked with the exception of part of a glove on one hand. Why the position of the coffins had changed and where the rest of the bodies had gone was unknown

Mr Smith went on to tell that a few years later, General Playfair, a member of a prominent local family, obtained permission to access the chamber. He did so, accompanied by two of his brothers, and under the supervision of Mr Smith. This time the coffins were all removed, checked and returned, and there were no bodies. When asked what had happened to the body of the girl, Mr Smith had replied that he did not know and that, as far as he was aware, the fact that the vault contained a burial chamber was a secret known by only a very small number of people.

The reporter then went on to interview Professor Heddle, who had been present when the chamber was opened in 1868. He advised that due to the time that had elapsed, he did not remember much about it, a statement that I find curious as I'm sure that even back in the 1860s, opening a secret burial chamber was not a regular occurrence! He did recall that the vault was found full of skulls. He advised that he inspected theses, and he considered this to be of more importance than the 'nonsense' the reporter had come to discuss. They found that all of the skulls had excellent teeth, with no signs of decay, and that several showed that the people would not have been able to turn their head due to a problem with the last vertebrae in the neck. Why so many skulls would be in the same place that all showed this unusual and rare condition could not be explained. He also advised that some of the skulls had the lower jaw tied closed with a handkerchief with a bleaching hole. He found this odd as this method of bleaching had only been discovered in the last two hundred years, yet there was no records within this time of the tower being used as a burial chamber.

The reporter put it to him that the bones were placed there by a sexton to which Professor Heddle replied that he could only see skulls. When asked what happened to the skulls, he advised they were taken to be placed in the museum, however, Principle Sharp objected and instructed they were to be returned. It seems they were instead thrown over the cliff edge into the sea below.

Professor Heddle confirmed that he returned a few days later for the opening of the sealed chamber (indicating the vault that contained the skulls was the one referred to by Mr Hall as containing the stairs that gave access to a sealed room). Within this chamber, he saw two coffins lying to the east and west, and the remainder were stacked in the middle of the room at right angles. Inside the coffin closest to him, he saw a body, but the head had been broken off. He also reached into one of the other coffins, and assessed it to contain the body of a man. He stated he did not remove any of the bodies and the entrance was again sealed. When asked if he knew what had happened to the bodies since, he replied that as far as he knew they were still there.

The final person the reporter interviewed was Mr D. Hay Fleming who, although just a child when the chamber was opened on 21st August 1868, had knowledge of a later opening in 1888, this time at the request of W.T. Linskill, who would later become the Dean of Guild of St Andrews. This time the chamber was found to be in a state of disarray, with the coffins mixed up and bone fragments scattered all over. Three coffins had been found to have been placed on trestles, which had partially collapsed, and one was noted to contain the body of a well preserved woman wearing a long glove on one hand.

Dean Linskill also wrote to many papers during 1894 about the reports regarding the tower. In the letter, he strongly refuted many of the stories, describing them as nonsense, and stated that he had heard the tales about the tower since he had been a child. He confirmed that when he entered the vault, it had been found to be in a disorderly state and one of the coffins had contained the body of a woman dressed in satin which, when touched, 'became dust'. On her hands, which are described as being skeletal (which seems to contradict the stories that the bodies were well preserved) she wore long white gauntlet gloves, with many buttons. At the time of the re-opening of the tomb, a stonemason named Grieve attended. He had been involved in the 1868 discovery of the chamber and commented that it now looked quite different from how it did then. Dean Linskill concluded that the chamber must have been accessed on numerous unreported occasions between 1868 and 1888 with the bodies and coffins being tampered with.

It is clear that the versions of what was found within the chamber vary, even with those present, and it is also apparent by the statements by some that they could not remember much, that there was a reluctance to say what they saw or to be involved in any of the subsequent speculation. The biggest question however must be what happened to the bodies between the various openings of the tomb? One can speculate that the bodies were completely removed at some point by an unknown person, only to be returned later, all without attracting the attention of the curious locals or the numerous people working at the cathedral. Not an easy task when you consider that it would involve creating an opening in a stone wall large enough for the bodies to fit through, and then repeating the process to return them. It does however seem Linskill was correct not only with his belief that the chamber had been opened several more times, but also that they it had actually been known about earlier as, while carrying out my research, I found a newspaper article from the *Dundee Courier* dated 3rd July 1861, seven years earlier than the much documented first discovery.

This 1861 report states that stonemasons working at the cathedral had removed some stones in one of the outer walls of a tower, believing it would give access to a continuation of the stair to the top of the wall. Instead, they discovered that the stairs led down to a burial chamber that contained several, well preserved bodies. It states that the entrance was immediately closed and work stopped pending advices from the department of Woods and Forests. There is no mention in this report of the inner doorway to the burial chamber being found to be sealed at this earliest discovery, and so when the article refers to the entrance being closed, it could well mean the doorway rather than the outer wall, indicating this could have been when the door was first sealed. Interestingly, the work was supervised by none other than a 'Mr Hall'.

This was quite possibly Mr Jessie Hall who, when interviewed for the *Telegraph* in 1894, initially seemed keen to quell the reporter's interest in the tower. It was only when pressed that he confirmed he had (reluctantly) allowed the burial chamber to be opened, yet he seemed to have known that there was an inner chamber with the stair and a blocked up doorway inside. To me, this seems to imply that when approached in 1868, he was dismissive as he already had prior knowledge of the contents and knew of the attention that re-opening the burial chamber would attract resulting in possible delays to the work he was overseeing. Any wall that may have formerly enclosed the stair is now gone, and metal gates prevent access to the chambers within the tower.

Recently, Historic Scotland were good enough to grant me permission to go inside these chambers, and my first observation would be that they are too small to have contained twelve coffins and that any suggestion that three of them had been set up on trestles would have to be completely dismissed. I did ask the member of staff who accompanied me, and he advised it was not the lower chamber the coffins were found, but the one above. This would appear to contradict the reporting, but as we have already seen, unfortunately the information given by those present at the initial openings cannot be relied upon. I commented that it was difficult to imagine so many coffins in such a small space, and was advised that they had been stood upright, leaning against the wall. I am grateful to Historic Scotland for allowing me to be one of a few people who have ever entered these chambers.

Reports of sightings of the White Lady persisted, and on 7th October, 1902, a story was published in the *Evening Post* titled 'The Fisherman's Story'. The tale was provided to the paper by an old fisherman who recalled that on a stormy night, his brother had been returning home from the harbour, on the path that leads past the haunted tower. As he approached he saw something white sticking out from the tower and as he got nearer, he saw it was a human arm. He rushed to help but as he reached out to grasp the hand, it immediately vanished.

Exterior of the Haunted Tower

My grandfather used to tell me a similar story concerning a gate that gives access to the cathedral just a short distance from the tower. These gates are locked at night and he told me that if you place your hands through the bars of the gate after dark, you will feel the faint touch of gloved hands on your arms. However, if you stay too long, the unseen hands will grab you and attempt to pull you through the gates. He omitted to ever say how long 'too long' was, and so it is something I have never tried!

Side Gate to Cathedral

Before moving on from this area, there is another location that is well worth a visit. On the seaward side of the cathedral, beside the haunted tower, sit the ruins of the church of St Mary on the Rock. This church dates back to the 12th century, although it is believed there was an earlier church on the same site that dated back to the 9th century, and was the church of the Culdees, a community of Celtic monks who refused to acknowledge the monastic orders introduced in the Middle Ages and chose to remain living alone. St Marys also acted as a college but, like the neighbouring cathedral, suffered significant damage during the reformation and little remains today.

The Remains of the Church of St Mary on the Rocks

Returning to the cathedral, it would seem appropriate at this stage to once again mention Dean W.T. Linskill. Not only was he heavily involved with the discoveries in the haunted tower mentioned earlier, he was also a great supporter of the theory that a number of underground passageways ran beneath the town, particularly between the cathedral and the castle. This belief is supported by the mine and countermine at the castle, which had long been forgotten and only rediscovered when, in 1879, the ground beneath a workman demolishing the old keepers cottage at the castle gave way, and he fell into the tunnel, along with his wheel barrow. This proved that the rock below ground was strong enough for a tunnel to be formed, and given the castle tunnels were dug in less than a year with basic tools, it also showed that it was possible for such tunnels to be cut. Linskill was granted permission on numerous occasions to dig in an attempt to find the tunnels, but was never successful. He followed all of the work at the cathedral while the ground was being cleared and lowered, confident that underground chambers would be found that would contain the cathedral's gold and jewels, which had never been accounted for, and possibly the entrance to the tunnels. It seemed however that he was always one step behind the workers, with numerous discoveries being made, including a small, narrow stair that is reported to have led down into a vaulted room (often referred to as 'the little stair' of the cathedral) but is seems it was filled in with the rubble that was being cleared from the site before Linskill could get there. On one such discovery of access to an underground room, the foreman is reported to have told the workers who discovered it to fill it in without exploring it stating it was 'just another' of these chambers. The potential amount of history and artefacts that may have been lost during this time is unimaginable.

Dean Linskill is however also well known for his knowledge of St Andrews ghost lore, on which he wrote two books, initially *The Strange Story of St Andrews Haunted Tower* and then, in 1911, *'St Andrews Ghost Stories'*. Despite his 1894 letter, previously referred to, in which he stated that 'ghost stories of the usual absurd kind are numerous', it seems Linskill very much came round to the idea of the tales of hauntings and it is rare that you will read anything covering the ghosts of St Andrews in any depth without the author at least referring to the work of Linskill. In his 1911 book, Linskill tells of a number of accounts of sightings of the White Lady, such as one relayed to him by 'an old friend', which reads:

'It must have been the end of January or the beginning of February, and I was strolling along to the Kirkhill after dinner and enjoying the fine evening and the keen sea breeze and thinking about the old, old days of the castle and the cathedral, of Beaton's ghost, and many other queer tales, when a female figure glided past me. She was in a long, flowing white dress, and had her beautiful dark hair hanging down past her waist. I was very much astonished to see a girl dressed in such a manner wandering about alone at such an hour, and I followed her along for several yards, when lo! Just after she had passed the turret light she completely vanished near the square tower, which I was afterwards informed was known as the 'Haunted Tower,' I hunted all round the place carefully, but saw nothing more that night.'

The book goes on to tell of a second sighting by the same man, this time with his sister present:

'It was a lovely night with a faint moon, and as the white lady swept past quite silently we saw the soft trailing dress and the long, black wavy hair. There was something like

a rosary hanging from her waist, and a cross or a locket hanging round her throat. As she passed she turned her head towards us, and we both noticed her beautiful features, especially her brilliant eyes. She vanished, as before, near that old tower. My sister was so awfully frightened that I had to hurry her off home. We were both absolutely convinced we had seen a being not of this world'

The gentleman proceeds to tell of a third sighting, when the White Lady appeared to him while he was staying in an old guest house. On this occasion he claimed to have followed the ghost to a painting in the gallery, where she vanished. When looking at the painting, he immediately recognised it to be of the ghost and he discovered it was of one of Mary, Queen of Scots, four Maries (Marys) the name given to her four ladies-in-waiting (who were all called Mary). He was informed that the lady in the picture had fallen in love with a French Minstrel, who was later executed at St Andrews, after which she became a nun and died at a young age. Further tales of the White Lady covered in the book refer to information provided to Linskill by 'a very dear old lady friend', who re-affirmed the story that the White Lady was one of the four Maries and referred him to a book that she had, titled *'The Queen's Maries'*, by G J Whyte-Melville, published in 1862. While I have no reason to doubt that Linskill was provided these stories in the manner stated, it seems he has taken them simply at face value. Notwithstanding the fact that someone would have to be incredibly lucky to see a rarely seen spirit on three separate occasions, some research confirmed that the book *'The Queen's Maries'* is a novel rather than a work of historical facts. In addition, the 'Marie' referred to as becoming a nun, who they believed to be the White Lady, is named as Mary Hamilton. Mary Hamilton was not however one of the Queen's Maries and only exists in the context of being a lady-in-waiting to a Scottish Queen in a ballad that tells a fictional tale of the execution of Mary Hamilton after she became pregnant to the King, and killed the baby. I therefore feel it is safe to say that the identity of the White Lady is not one of the four Maries.

I am however lucky enough to have been provided with an eye witness account of a sighting for this book. A lady named Pauline told me that while she was a child, she lived close to the cathedral. One dark evening, at around 10pm, she watched as the White Lady walked along the section of cathedral wall closest to the sea, towards the Haunted Tower, before disappearing. It is curious that several people have reported to have seen the spectre walking the wall as, in these far less equal times, it would be very unlikely that a woman would be allowed on the defensive walls as access would be restricted to the friars and the guards. Despite this, for her spirit to be seen on the walls, it is fair to conclude that in life the White Lady was in some way connected to the wall, which just adds to the mystery of her identity.

The Haunted Tower is not the only tower associated with ghosts in the Cathedral, St Rule's tower is reported to be haunted by the phantom of a friendly monk.

St Rule's Tower (also known as St Regulus Tower and the Square Tower)

An incident frequently mentioned in publications is said to have occurred in the early 1950s when a visitor to the town was climbing the steep steps of the tower and stumbled. He grabbed the handrail and managed to steady himself and when he looked back up to continue his ascent, he saw a man further up the steps, dressed in what appeared to be a cassock. Any thoughts that the visitor had regarding the man's unusual choice of clothing were forgotten when the friendly soul asked if he was all right, and offered his arm to help him up the worn stairs. The visitor politely declined the man's offer of assistance and continued on his way, passing him as he did so. Upon reaching the top of the tower, he found he was alone and, after taking in the views, he returned to the bottom and again passed nobody. By now, his curiosity about the helpful figure that he had encountered had returned. He had been aware of just how narrow the tight spiral staircase was during his descent, yet he did not recall having to walk tightly to one side while passing the man, nor brushing against him, and he began to wonder how he could have passed the man on the stairs with such ease. Seeing one of the custodians outside the tower, the visitor asked about the other man and was shocked to learn that no-one else had entered or left the tower. The custodian however was quick to re-assure him that he had simply encountered the phantom monk of the tower, a helpful ghost who often appears to assist those who struggle with the stairs.

This spook is believed to be the spirit of Robert of Montrose, a canon of the church who was elected Prior of St Andrews around 1387. Montrose was a popular prior, described in the 1838 book *'History of St Andrews, Ancient and Modern'* by the Rev C. J. Lyon, M.A. as being 'respectful to his seniors, mild to his juniors, gentle to his religious brethren, unyielding to the proud and obstinate, condescending to the humble, and tender-hearted to the penitent'. It is also stated that he 'did not flatter the great nor fear their threats; he did not oppress the poor, but protected them'. Despite his popularity, one young monk under his supervision, named Thomas Platter, showed little respect to him or to the church. Montrose refused to give up on Platter, who is described in the Rev. Lyon's book as being an 'undisciplined and unruly' man, and he continued to try to help the young man before, eventually, confining him to a cell for two days in the hope that would give him the time to see the error of his ways. Unfortunately, it seems while Montrose was spending time believing that there was good in everyone, Platter's mind had turned to ways to rid himself of the good prior.

In 1393, as Montrose climbed the stairs from the cloister to the dormitory, something he did every night, Platter followed in the darkness and pulled out a dagger before attacking the prior and fatally wounding him.

The Night Stair on which Robert of Montrose was murdered

Montrose survived but lived for just three days before succumbing to his injuries and dying. He had however been able to identify his assailant before his death and Platter was captured while trying to escape the monastery. Two days after the funeral of Robert of Montrose, Platter stood trial for the murder in front of the Bishop Walter Trail and, inevitably, he was found guilty and sentenced to be forever imprisoned on a diet of just bread and water. In reality, this was a death sentence. The church was not permitted to formally carry out executions and to do so they would have had to hand Platter over to the civil authorities. Preferring to keep matters within the church, by placing the murderous monk on insufficient rations he would either become too weak to fight disease in the unsanitary conditions of the prison cell, or he would starve to death. Platter did indeed die not long after his incarceration, and rather than being laid to rest in consecrated ground, he was buried in a dung heap.

Despite his violent death, it seems the spirit of Robert of Montrose remains loyal to his beliefs and that he continues to offer assistance to those in need of help. As for Thomas Platter, there is a tale told locally that when the work began to clear the cathedral site in the nineteenth century, that his figure began to be seen walking in the grounds of the cathedral. In 1898, he appeared in front of a catholic worker and identified himself before pleading for his remains to be given a Christian burial. It was soon discovered that bones had in fact been disturbed during the work at the cathedral, around the time the ghost of Thomas Platter first started to appear. The bones are said to have been given a proper burial in the Cathedral cemetery and no further sightings of Thomas Platter have been made. Unfortunately there seems to be no record of this burial in the news archives and so this story can only be classed as ghost-lore.

There are also reports of a figure being seen either standing at the top of the square tower looking over the edge or falling from it. For a long time this was believed to also be Robert of Montrose, as he was known to enjoy climbing the tower and gazing at the views, and a variation of his murder told that Platter had in fact stabbed him at the top of the tower and threw his body over the edge. Recently, as the details of the murder have become widely available to more people, this version of events can be discounted, but the question remains, if the figure seen at the top of the tower and falling from its heights isn't Robert of Montrose, who is he? While carrying out the research for this book, I found an almost unknown story that may provide the answer.

This tale of a love triangle with tragic consequences was published in the

Evening Post newspaper on 26th May 1900 under the heading, 'The St Regulus Tower Mystery'. According to the article, two men, Henry Ferguson and John Munro had been students at St Andrews University many years prior. Both were older men and so distanced themselves from the usual student antics, which ended up bringing them together. Rather than bonding, they developed a mutual dislike for each other that spurred them on to compete against each other, resulting in both excelling academically. As their time at University neared an end, they came up against each other in a college scholarship competition, which Munro ultimately won. Unhappy with this outcome, it seems Ferguson somehow managed to persuade the authorities that Munro had cheated, which resulted in the scholarship being withheld and Munro eventually expelled from the University.

This was to have far reaching consequences for Munro as, not only was his academic career over, news soon reached his intended bride, Helen Ward, who subsequently refused to see him. It seems this news was almost certainly brought to Miss Ward by Ferguson, as when Munro, ashamed and broken hearted, left the town shortly after to take up work on a nearby estate, Ferguson made his move on Miss Ward, and they were soon believed to be a couple. After two years the town was full of gossip that they were to be married, however, Miss Ward suddenly took her own life by throwing herself into the cold, dark waters of the Step Rock. The reason for this tragic act seemed to be Ferguson telling her that rather than intending to marry her, he was tired of her and was planning to leave the country without her.

Upon hearing the tragic news, Munro returned to the town the same day and her family allowed him in to see her body. Seeing how her appearance had changed during her time with Ferguson, Munro was filled with guilt that soon turned to anger. At the funeral, Ferguson is said to have followed the coffin with his head bowed, not raising it until Miss Ward's body was lowered into her grave at St Andrews Cathedral. His eyes immediately met with Munro's and, filled with horror to see his foe had returned, he swiftly left the cemetery.

Later that night, unable to sleep and filled with guilt, Ferguson felt compelled to visit the Step Rock where, as he gazed over the waters in which Miss Ward had perished, he became aware he was not alone. He turned to see Munro had also come to the Step Rock. Ferguson asked what he wanted and Munro simply demanded that Ferguson follow him. Something in the way he looked seemed to convince Ferguson to do as he was told, and he allowed Munro to lead him up the steep path from the Step Rock and along the coastal path, eventually reaching the cathedral gate, which Munro opened. Ferguson pleaded for them to talk outside without the need to enter the graveyard, but Munro simply indicated to him to enter, which he did. He was then led to the bottom of St Rules Tower where Munro opened the door and waited for Ferguson to enter. Again he resisted, repeating his request that they talk outside, but this time he saw something glinting in Munro's hand. Recognising it as a pistol, he knew his best chance was to do as he was asked in the hope they could talk things through.

When they reached the top of the tower, Munro broke his silence and exploded with rage. He demanded that Ferguson look over the edge of the tower, down upon the fresh mound of soil that marked the grave of Miss Ward. He urged him to think back over his actions of the last few years, first destroying Munro's college career before stealing the woman he loved and then driving her to her death. Finally, he told Ferguson that he had brought him here to fulfil a promise he made to Miss Ward at her graveside, to avenge her death and to kill him. Ferguson realised that he could not overpower Munro while he still had the pistol, and instead pleaded for his life. To his surprise, Munro threw a pistol towards him, and explained he had brought two. Rather than simply murder Ferguson, Munro challenged him to a duel. Ferguson seemed to have again found a glimmer of hope in the situation in which he had found himself, and pointed out that whoever wins will subsequently be hung for murder, making it pointless, but Munro explained he had thought of that. They were to stand back to back at the centre of the tower roof and, upon the command, they would both walk to opposite sides, climb upon the wall that surrounds the roof, before turning and firing. The body of the loser would fall to the ground, and the injuries caused by the impact would hide all signs of the gunshot wound. With limited scope for medical examinations, the true cause of death would never be discovered. Ferguson accepted, and the two men stood back to back, as agreed, before starting to walk towards the opposite walls.

Suddenly, Munro heard a shot ring out and he felt a bullet graze his shoulder. Instead of honouring the rules of a duel, Ferguson had opted to try to shoot him in the back, but missed (duelling pistols from that time are known to have been remarkably inaccurate). Rather than risk turning his back again, Munro ordered Ferguson to climb upon the wall as he watched, before backing up himself, taking his position on the wall opposite and shouting 'Fire!' Both men fired their pistols, with Ferguson again missing but he was not so lucky himself and he was hit. Stumbling backwards, he lost his footing and plummeted from the top of the tower, crying out as he did so, before there was a solid 'thud' as he hit the ground. Munro calmly picked up Ferguson's pistol, which he had dropped, and descended the tower stairs, only pausing briefly to once again look at the grave of Miss Ward before leaving the scene.

In the morning, when Ferguson's body was found and, as expected, the gunshot wound was not noticed among the numerous other visible injuries on his broken and bloodied body. The townsfolk assumed that, unable to cope with the loss of his sweetheart, he had taken his own life. Munro meanwhile joined the army and was killed several years later in battle, leaving his diaries that covered this tragic time of his life, from which the reporter had pieced together the story for publication.

Without any dates, it is very difficult to find facts that would substantiate this story. There are no death records or newspaper articles that I have been able to find using just the names and locations, although the possibility that the names were changed for the article to protect family members cannot be ruled out. The *Dundee Courier* did promote the story on the same day, stating it was a true story and, assuming it was, this could give the identity of the figure seen peering from the top of the tower, just as Ferguson had when he was forced to look down over Miss Ward's grave, before being seen falling to his death.

The Square Tower is well worth a visit and, on a clear day, you can view the surrounding countryside for miles around. As you enter, you will note that there is an old bell hanging beside the door. Local legend tells that ringing the bell lets the spirit of Robert of Montrose know you are entering and the friendly monk will be waiting for you inside to offer assistance. Ring it if you dare!

The bell at the door of St Rule's Tower

On the 3rd of August 1904, the *Dundee Courier* published an article telling of another spooky bell story connected to the Cathedral. Taken from the writing of Rev C. J. Lyon, M.A. regarding the history of St Andrews, the tale tells that when the destruction of St Andrews Cathedral first started, the bells were removed from the steeple and loaded onto a boat to be exported from Scotland. It explains that this was not an uncommon deed, and during the Reformation vast quantities of lead and bell metal were taken from the religious houses, records of which can be found in the Vatican library in Rome. Tragedy was however to follow the attempts to steal the bells from St Andrews and the ship carrying them sank in the bay, within sight of the steeple from which they had been taken. Although the bells were never recovered, on certain days it is said that they can still be heard ringing from beneath the waves.

The Cathedral can also lay claim to its own version of 'Greyfriars Bobby', the Skye terrier who, after his master's death, loyally guarded his grave in Greyfriars Kirkyard for fourteen years, winning the heart of the Edinburgh townsfolk, before his own passing on 14th January 1872. The phantom dog in St Andrews Cathedral is less fortunate, as it is said to only have three legs. Although documentation is somewhat scarce, it seems this black dog has been witnessed over a very long period of time. Had the tale merely been that a black dog has been seen in the Cathedral over the years, I would consider there no story to tell as it is only relatively recently that the gates have been locked overnight to prohibit access, before which the public could wander the site at all hours, sometimes while exercising their dogs. The dog having only three legs however sparked some interest in the claimed sightings, as for a three legged dog to be seen over the many years (meaning there would have had to be successive generations of three legged dogs) is far less difficult to explain.

But why is the dog seen in the Cathedral grounds? The answer to that may lie in an almost unknown section of the cemetery, described in an article headed, 'Burial Place of Faithful Friends', published in the *Evening Telegraph* on 12th May 1964 as being a 'unique spectacle' in a shaded nook on the south side of the cemetery, hidden among the flowers, sits a small dog cemetery. A number of headstones are reported to mark the deceased pets, of which there are a total of seven named, which died between 11th September 1892 and November 11th 1903. Although little more is known about them, it is possible that the three legged dog seen in the cathedral is one of these beloved companions searching for its master.

Despite extensive searching and enquiries with Historic Scotland, I have been unable to locate these little headstones and so it seems they may have unfortunately been lost to time, which is quite possible as several plots in both the Cathedral Cemetery and the Eastern Cemetery (see next chapter) no longer have headstones and some of those that remain are too badly weathered to be read. Another possibility is that the article confused the dog cemetery at St Leonards School, which stands in the former grounds of the monastery, with the cathedral cemetery.

THE EASTERN CEMETERY

To the south east of the cathedral ground, a small gateway gives access to the Eastern Cemetery, an extension to the cathedral cemetery with the earliest legible headstone dating burials here as far back as 1823.

General view of the Eastern Cemetery

To say this place is haunted is probably something many readers would not find an unusual statement, however, contrary to popular perceptions, it is relatively rare for a cemetery to be actively haunted. As we have already seen throughout this book, hauntings either seem to take place where there has been a sudden or violent death, or in a place where a deceased person had very strong ties. A cemetery, in contrast, is a place of peace and tranquillity, a place where bodies are placed after the death, a final resting place. That is not to say cemeteries are never haunted, several ghost tales connected with the cathedral cemetery have already been covered, although these are associated with murder and mystery within the grounds themselves. That said, there is a general belief, particularly in Scottish folklore, that most cemeteries do have one spirit, a guardian who remains hidden while overlooking the wellbeing of the other tombs. The identity of the guardian spirit is not normally known, although in the eastern cemetery, it is more visible than most.

In an elevated position at the top of the cemetery, a large stone angel holding a cross and gazing up at the sky marks one of the earliest graves, and many believe that it is this angel that protects the sacred ground around it.

Angel Statue

Although not a traditional ghost, there have been reports of bursts of energy from the cemetery which people have felt even while walking up the street outside the cemetery walls, but most curiously, the angel is said to move, with claims being made of a white, winged figure being seen moving around in the darkness.

I was first told the story of the angel as a relatively young child, one evening just as it was turning dark and, at the time, it terrified me. Not so much because of the content of the story, but there is some physical anomalies with this otherwise pristine statue that would seem to support the claims. A close look at her right hand would seem to show its position on the cross has changed several times, with the clear outline of both the lower part of the hand and the little finger in a different spot.

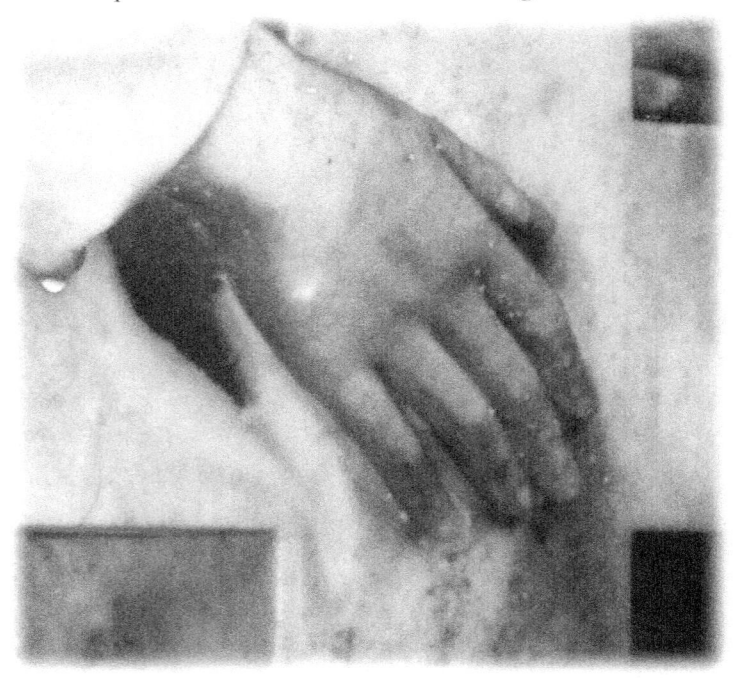

Angel's hand showing where it appears the finger used to rest

It is difficult to say what has caused this, perhaps it as an error made by the stone mason or perhaps it is differential weathering, with a section of the cross being protected by the carved hand. Or maybe the tales are true and, rather than a phantom, the animated stone angel does indeed walk the grounds at night.

THE PENDS AND THE HARBOUR

Leaving the Eastern Cemetery via the gate at the bottom of the hill, you will enter a road known as 'The Pends'. Running from the harbour to South Street, passing through a double gateway with a once vaulted roof at the top and a single gateway at the bottom, the Pends forms one of the oldest remaining routes into the city, dating back as far as the mid-1300s. Turning left from the Eastern Cemetery and through the single gateway will take you to the harbour, a place well worth a visit in its own right. Dating back to the Middle Ages, the importance of the harbour has been acknowledged by Historic Scotland who have placed a category 'A' listing on the structures, the highest level of listing possible.

The original medieval pier was rebuilt in stone in 1559 and, over the centuries, underwent some re-modelling, either to repair storm damage or to extend its length. This included using stone from the cathedral and castle following their demise. A concrete terminal pillar was added to the end of the pier in 1900. The shorter cross pier provides further protection to the harbour and lock gates to create the inner harbour were installed in 1728.

General view of the harbour

This is still a working harbour and it is not uncommon to see the fishermen landing their catch of crabs and lobsters from their boats. Another common sight if visiting on a Sunday, around midday, is the students walking along the length of the pier in their red gowns. This walk, known as 'the pier walk' has been a tradition in the town for many years, with the students meeting in St Salvator's Quad after attending church, and walking along the lower, wider section of the pier, before climbing the ladder at the end to walk back along the narrower upper section. It is believed that the students do not always make this walk alone, with the figure of a man being witnessed at the end of the pier, sometimes described as being in full form and other times as being merely a ghostly shadow. This phantom is said to walk back along the pier with the students, matching their pace if they try to speed up to get away. Among those who have encountered this spook is the novelist, screenwriter and journalist, Fay Weldon, who studied Economics and Psychology at the University of St Andrews. In an article she wrote titled 'My glimpses of the afterlife mean I no longer fear death', published in the *Daily Mail* on 22nd May 2013 she tells of her experience and how she has now come to accept what took place on the pier in 1951. Describing the man that she encountered as wearing a preacher's hat and 'winking in and out of nothingness', she tells that the local legend says that this is the ghost of a parson from Dundee, but who drowned at the pier while on his way to preach to the students in 1551. In her book, '*Auto Da Fay*' published by Harper Collins in 2002, she theorises whether the tradition of the pier walk is the reason the pastor continues to remain in this world, with the students walk on a Sunday preventing his spirit from making the separation needed for him to move on.

The Pends Gateway from the Harbour

THE NEW INNS

Returning through the gateway to The Pends, a high stone wall to the left hides some of the buildings which make up St Leonards Private School. An arched gateway from The Pends giving access to the grounds is in fact an ancient entrance constructed to give access to a far older building on the site named the Hospitum Novum, or the New Inns.

Gateway to the former New Inns

Various hauntings are said to have taken place within the walls of the New Inns, although there does not seem to be any specific reason why or any connection between them. It seems the building was destined to be cursed from the start, with tradition telling that it was hastily constructed (some reports state within a month), in 1537 to provide accommodation for Madeleine of Valois, the first bride of King James V. Madeleine, the daughter of King Francis I of France, had been a poorly child, so much so that she had been raised away from Paris in the valley of the River Loire. King Francis originally resisted her marriage to James, fearing that the Scottish climate would be detrimental to her health. James persisted, and when Madeleine told her father that she too wished to marry James, he reluctantly allowed it to go ahead. They were married on 1st January 1537 at Notre Dame Cathedral in Paris, before setting sail for Scotland in May, by which time Madeleine's health had suffered as a result of the months of celebrations. This may be what prompted King James instructing that a residence away from Edinburgh should be constructed to allow his bride to recover. St. Andrews no doubt was chosen as an ideal location for the residence due to its fresh sea air and the ready built defences, with the New Inns being built within the walls of the monastery grounds. Unfortunately when the ship carrying the royal couple arrived in Leith from France on 19th May, the queen's health had worsened and she died on 7th July 1537, just before her 17th birthday, at the Palace of Holyroodhouse in Edinburgh, having never visited St. Andrews. King James was still to use the building as a residence for his queen, with it said to have been refurbished and used for the reception of his second wife, Mary of Guise, who arrived in Fife from France in June 1538, less than a year after the death of Madeleine.

The New Inns continued to house Royal visitors, with some reports claiming that Mary, Queen of Scots, were among the guests and it later became the residence for the Archbishops. One curious tale relates to James Sharp, a deeply unpopular character in St. Andrews history who held the position of Archbishop from 1661 until his murder in 1679. During his time as Archbishop, he had been at Edinburgh overseeing the prosecution of some Covenanters captured at Pentland, when he realised he had left some papers containing vital information in his residence at the New Inns. He summoned his footman and gave him clear instructions on the location of the papers in a cabinet before giving him the key and sending him on his way. The footman made good time, reaching St. Andrews in just six hours. When he arrived, he was surprised when he opened the door to the room to see the Archbishop sitting near the window, wearing his distinctive black gown and broad hat. Conscious of Sharp's temper, the footman tried to make light of the situation by congratulating him on the speed of his ride, commenting that he was sure he had seen the Archbishop in Edinburgh that morning, and that it was a wonder he did not see him pass on the way to St. Andrews. Sharp did not answer, and merely turned and stared at the young man with a look of displeasure. The footman rushed downstairs to alert the Steward that the Archbishop was in residence, and was unhappy. The Steward refused to believe him, stating that no-one had entered the building. The footman's persistence persuaded him to join him to look and, upon reaching the bottom of the stairs, they both saw Sharp standing at the top of the stairs, looking angrily towards them, which frightened them enough to not dare go up. A short while later the footman ventured upstairs, hoping that the Archbishop had calmed down, but instead he found there was nobody there. He hurriedly gathered the papers as he had been instructed and made his way back to Edinburgh as quickly as he could. When he met Sharp, and handed him the papers, he made comment about the incident at the New Inns and was told by the Archbishop, in no uncertain terms, that he must never talk of what he saw.

While the logical answer to this tale is that the Archbishop had made his way to St. Andrews and back as well, possibly to carry out some task that he did not want witnessed, hence telling the footman he must never talk of it, it would be odd for him to instruct the footman to make the journey at the same time and to be in the same place, where it was almost inevitable he would be seen. Equally strange if he had been in St. Andrews, is that he did not collect the papers himself. There are plentiful tales of ghosts of the living being seen through the centuries, often as a forewarning and, although it is impossible to date this incident other than it must have been sometime after the Pentland Rising of the Covenanters in 1666, perhaps Archbishop Sharp did not want it mentioned as he recognised it as a warning of his own pending doom, something his enemies would have no doubt used to their advantage.

Another tale relating to Archbishop Sharp and most probably the New Inns involve a witch trial which he was overseeing. An Edinburgh woman named Janet Douglas had been accused of witchcraft and consulting with evil spirits. When these allegations were made to her, she denied all charges against her but claimed that she knew who the real witches were as, rather than being one, she had been pursuing them in an attempt to undermine their plots. It seems this was in fact a warning to Sharp, although he either did not recognise it as such or did not take it seriously and kept pressing for a confession from the woman. In reply, she is said to have simply asked Sharp who it was that has been in his 'closet' (the same room referred to in the tale of his living ghost at the New Inns) on Saturday night between midnight and 1am. It is claimed Sharp 'turned black and pale' at that stage, and nothing else was said.

The Duke of Rothesay, who was also on the counsel for the trial, called Janet to a side room, and asked who she had seen the Archbishop with, to which she replied 'My Lord, it was a muckle (large) black devil'. The remaining details of the trial are not recorded, although it is known that Janet Douglas was banished to the plantations, an extremely lenient punishment for those accused of witchcraft who rarely escape with their life, and so it would seem that the authorities had been keen to stop her revealing what she knew.

A tale of two more spectres at the New Inns is told in a letter to the Reverend Robert Wodrow, dated 14th January 1718. The letter reveals that the writer's brother in law, Andrew Berrage, had been principle servant to Bishop Rose (also known as Ross), Archbishop of St. Andrews from 1684 to 1689, during which time he resided at the New Inns. Berrage told his sister and the writer that there was a room in the dwelling that no-one would stay in due to the apparitions that appeared there. On one occasion there had been so many visitors at the property, that there was no option but to use the room, and a young man was unlucky enough to be given the haunted chamber. In order to try to dispel the beliefs, Barrage offered to stay the night with the guest in the room. Having lit a fire in the fireplace to keep the room light and warm, they turned in for the night. With only one bed in the room, the two men lay back to back, with Berrage facing the door and the visitor facing the opposite side of the room.

Around midnight, while both men were still awake, the figure of a coachman appeared in full form at the door while at the opposite side of the room a postilion (who would have ridden one of the front horses of a horse drawn carriage to aid with the steering) appeared. Berrage shouted out to the coachman, accusing him of being drunk and telling him that he should be in bed at such an hour. The coachman did not reply, but merely started to walk towards the bed. The postilion also started to advance towards them.

Berrage became angry at the coachman's actions and rose before swinging a punch at him, only to find that his clenched fist passed straight through the figure as though no-one was there. Both figures then started to move back towards their corners of the room, and vanished.

Berrage dropped to the floor in prayer, after which both men, having composed themselves, discussed what they had seen and after agreeing to tell no-one of their encounter, they spent the rest of the night in front of the fire. Inevitably, word got out and spread among the other servants and eventually Archbishop Ross heard of the encounter. Having become increasingly frustrated at the rumours, he decided to stay in the room himself to end the idle gossip once and for all. Berrage opted to sleep in the room below and just after midnight he heard noises from above, before witnessing the bishop run down the stairs still in his night gown, calling on his servants, but refusing to say what had disturbed him so much that he had fled the room.

Guests continued to report uncomfortable feelings, noise disturbances, items being moved around and phantom figures being seen, with the energy force seemingly growing over the years to the extent that people were so terrified they refused to stay and the building was eventually completely demolished at the start of the 1800s.

THE NUNS WALK

At the top of the Pends, just before the double arched gateway, a small lane leading off to the side is the haunt of one of the most feared ghosts in St. Andrews. Known as The Nuns Walk, the lane leads to St Leonards Chapel, a small parish church that has been in use since 1413.

The Nuns Walk

The tale behind this ghost, referred to as either 'The Veiled Lady', or 'The Veiled Nun', is a classic tale of love and tragedy. Centuries ago, it is said a young woman lived in the town, who was not only intelligent and wealthy with strong religious beliefs; she was also blessed with great beauty. As would be expected, she attracted the interest of many men, all keen to take her hand in marriage, however, she showed no interest and turned them all away until eventually, one suitor caught her eye and they were soon engaged to be married. What happened next varies, some say that her fiancé died in a tragic accident, others say he called off the marriage, while the final version of the story is that the woman herself called off the wedding. Whatever happened, whether through a broken heart or to prevent her fiancé from pursuing her, the actions taken by the young woman remain consistent, with a sharp knife, she cut off her eyelids and her lips, sliced her nose from both nostrils and sliced or branded her cheeks, before turning to religion and becoming a nun. Due to the severity of her disfigurement, she wore a veil for the remainder of her life and even in death; she continues to wander the chapel grounds. The story is disputed by many who are quick to point out that St Andrews never had a nunnery, but this did not mean there were no nuns in St Andrews. In the book *'Handbook to St. Andrews and Neighbourhood'* by David Hay Fleming, published by J & G Innes in 1897, the description of St Leonard's College buildings are given as follows:

'These are reached by a short lane which leaves South Street between Abbey Street and the Pends. So many pilgrims were attracted by the miracle-working relics of St Andrew, that a large hospital had to be built for their accommodation, so early, it seems, as the twelfth century. But in course of time the relics lost their virtue, the stream of pilgrims ceased to flow, and the Hospital of St Leonard was turned into a nunnery for old women. As they, however, showed no great regard either for morality or piety, it was changed into a College, in 1512, by Archbishop Alexander Stuart and Prior John Hepburn.'

It is therefore apparent that the college was formerly a nunnery, albeit a short-term make shift use of the building, which would place the time of the sad tale of the veiled lady to be in the early 1500s, which would match the story as told by Dean W.T. Linskill who stated the mutilation took place 'nearly 400 years ago' in his 1911 book, *St. Andrews Ghost Stories*. In this book he describes the haunting as follows:

'Her spirit with the terribly marred and mutilated face still wanders o' nights in the peaceful little avenue to old St Leonards iron kirk gate down the Pends Road. She is all dressed in black, with a long black veil over the once lovely face, and carries a lantern in her hand. Should any bold visitor to that avenue meet her, she slowly sweeps her face veil aside, raises the lantern to her scarred face, and discloses those awful features to his horrified gaze.'

The sight of the veiled lady's face is said to be sufficient to drive you insane, with a sighting as recent as the 1960s being recalled in an article named, 'The City of Souls' written by Annie Harrower-Gray and published in *the Scotland Magazine* in April 2010, which tells us that after seeing the ghost, a student was found slumped over stones in the lane, repeatedly saying 'the nun, the nun', until he was taken to a psychiatric hospital.

In other reports of the haunting, those who encounter the ghost are more fortunate with experiences including a feeling of being watched, the feeling of an invisible energy passing through you as you walk along the lane or simply a feeling of complete foreboding, which is sufficient to make people take an alternative route rather than walk through the lane. It seems it is not just humans that can sense this, an article in the online magazine, *'The Hazel Tree'*, tells that a dog owner had been walking her two terriers, which had been happily playing throughout the walk. When they reached the lane, the dogs suddenly stopped and cowered, whining at something invisible as it passed them.

Why the veiled lady appears in full form to some but not to others is a question that is unlikely to ever be discovered. My grandfather worked on the restoration of St Leonard's Chapel and, although he told that they did discover several bones during the work, he never reported any unusual feelings or sightings around the chapel or the Nuns Walk. In addition, hundreds of pupils from St Leonard's school walk along the lane every day without incident, and so it seems the nun is very selective in who she reveals herself to. With that said, most St. Andreans' still opt to avoid the lane at night rather than take the risk.

St Leonard's Chapel

OTHER GHOSTS OF THE PENDS

Despite the short length of the Pends, there are yet more ghosts said to lurk in the shadows of this walled road. A dark figure has been witnessed towards the top of the road, with those who encounter it only becoming aware when they enter the formerly roofed section of the Pends and they hear the sound of footsteps echo from behind. Those who turn have seen the figure on the opposite side of the road, and notice it matches their pace yet, as soon as they exit the gateway and look back, there is no-one to be seen. The description of the figure matching the pace of those it follows is similar to the preacher of the pier, and so it is possible this is the same spirit.

Double Archway giving access from South Street to The Pends

The rumbling sound wheels on the formerly cobbled road are also heard, before the distinctive shape of Archbishop Sharp's coach, pulled by four massive black horses emerge from the darkness. Curiously, despite the coach being heard, the horse's hooves are said to be silent. Archbishop Sharp will be discussed in more detail later, although for this part of his story it should be mentioned that his unpopularity and barbaric acts had been sufficient to lead many to believe he was in league with the Devil.

When he was murdered in 1679, travelling down the Pends would have been the final stage of his journey, had he made it. Those who are close enough to the coach say they see the terrified face of Archbishop Sharp pressed against the glass, with a darker figure sitting beside him with his hand resting on the Archbishop's shoulder. This second figure is widely believed to be the devil himself and rather than turn into the gateway of the New Inn, which would have been Sharp's final destination, the coach rushes through the sea gate before plunging into the harbour, with the devil said to be personally taking Sharp to Hell.

The final spirit of the Pends is somewhat bizarre. A pig has been reported running down the road. Those who have seen it are horrified to watch as it turns to look at them, revealing that the creature has human eyes. According to a report in the book *'A Ghost a Day'*, by Maureen Wood and Ron Kolek, published by F+W Media Inc. in 2010, the eyes are described as being 'full of despair, sadness, guilt and shame', and that the pig appears to be begging for understanding and compassion. The origin of this ghost remains a mystery to this day, but this has not prevented reports of sightings being passed down through generations meaning it cannot be ignored.

Despite all of the apparently negative spirits that lurk in The Pends, there is one part considered locally to give good luck, assuming that is what you desire. This is at the top, in an archway formed to allow access to the pavement of South Street, where it is said if you make a wish as you walk through, and keep that wish a secret, it will come true.

The 'Wishing' Archway

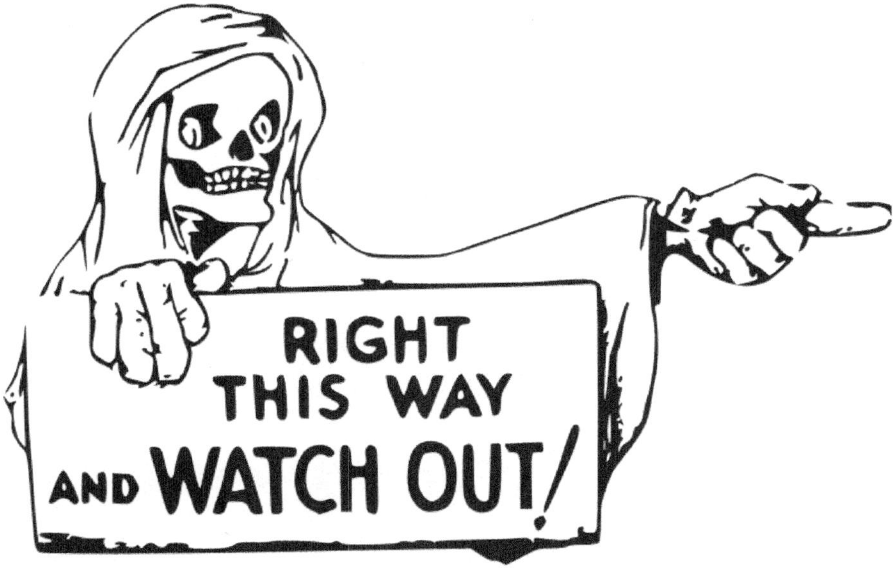
RIGHT
THIS WAY
AND WATCH OUT!

THE TOWN CENTRE

1) Deans Court
2) Queen Mary's House
3) St Leonard's House
4) The Byre Theatre
5) St May's College
6) Pontius Pilate
7) Blackfriars Chapel
8) Greyfriars Garden
9) The Cinema House
10) St Salvator's Chapel
11) The McIntosh Halls

DEANS COURT

Once outside the archway of the Pends, it is worth pausing to observe some of the buildings in this corner of the town, including the Roundel on the opposite side of the road, so called due to its circular corner tower.

The Roundel

Like many of the ancient buildings in the town, this 16th century former town house is now owned and preserved by St. Andrews University and is used as a study centre. Behind the Roundel sits Deans Court, a building dating back to the 15th century that is arguably the oldest dwelling house in St. Andrews, now providing accommodation for students. Like the cathedral, Deans Court is said to have a phantom dog. To add to the peculiarity of this spook, Deans Court has been refurbished many times with the floor levels being altered over the centuries, yet the dog still runs at the original floor level, which was several inches higher than the current level, making it appear to be floating.

Deans Court

Sightings of the dog in the courtyard, which has also been lowered, are recalled in an article titled 'Dog's Ghost on the Level', published in the *Dundee Courier and Advertiser* on 17th April 1948. The report covers a talk given by Professor John Reid in which he told that on moonlight nights, the dog can be seen running six inches above the courtyard, representing the higher ground level from the time when the dog was alive.

QUEEN MARY'S HOUSE

Returning to South Street and continuing into the town you will pass a row of three storey terraced houses. Nothing appears extraordinary about them until number 4 is viewed from the back, where it has a far more impressive appearance. This building, which was originally built between 1520 and 1526, sits on a site that has been occupied since the 12th century. Mary, Queen of Scots, is believed to have visited and stayed at the house a total of three times between 1560 and 1565, and the bedroom in which she stayed remains much as it was then for interested visitors to view. Other famous guests that have stayed at the house include Mary's great grandson, King James II, and Dr Samuel Johnson, the author of the first comprehensive English language dictionary. The house remained a private residence until 1926 when St Leonards School purchased it and remodelled it as a library, which was officially opened in 1927 by the Duchess of York (later the Queen Mother), and it remains in use as a library today.

The rear of Queen Mary's House

In 1977 a short guide book named *'Queen Mary's House and Those Who Lived In It'* was published by The Council of St Leonards School. The penultimate chapter, titled 'Recollections of Queen Mary's', written by Marjory Playfair Hannay, a member of a prominent St Andrews family, tells of her personal knowledge of some of the ghosts of the house. She recalls that Queen Mary's House was occupied by a lady named Mrs Thomson, who lived there with her mother until 1916, it was recognised that there were several tales of ghostly happenings within the walls of the house, two of which she was prepared to personally vouch for.

It is said that in the period before the First World War, many of the larger properties in St. Andrews were rented out over summer as holiday homes; Queen Mary's being one of them. A family from the South arrived, having arranged to stay at the house for the month of August, however, after just one week, they appeared at the office of the solicitor who was handling the letting, informed them they could no longer stay at the house and, after paying in full for the entire month, they left offering no explanation. Mrs Thomson had been somewhat confused by the families odd actions and what would cause them to refuse to stay at the house, but she soon got her answers while attending a function at a friend's house. It transpired that another guest knew the family who had stayed at Queen Mary's in August and, having learned that Mrs Thomson would be attending, she was keen to meet with her. She explained to Mrs Thomson that her friends had told them that while staying at the house, they had just sat down for dinner when the figure of a tall man wearing highland dress appeared out of a full length mirror. Without as much as a sideways glance, the figure walked silently across the room before disappearing through the door. This had disturbed them so much they were unable to stay at the house and left immediately.

Another phantom of the house was witnessed by Mrs Thomson and several other people, presumably at different times. In the library, a room below Queen Mary's room, a short scruffy looking man has been seen desperately trying to get at something in the corner. Unfortunately it seems no investigations have been carried out to see if there is anything in the wall at this part of the house which may offer an explanation for the figure, and no further details are offered on the spook.

In 1916, Captain Nunneley bought the house and moved in with his family. Although a friendly and hospitable family, Mrs Playfair Hannay states that they made it clear that they believed ghosts 'had no place in Queen Mary's', presumably meaning they had no belief in the supernatural. It seems at the time their views had however not yet influenced their young children, particularly their daughter Catherine, who would frequently ask her nanny about the identity of the funny looking old man wearing a brown dressing gown, who used to walk around the garden that their nursery overlooked, reading a book. Whenever the nanny checked, there was never anyone in the garden.

The final tale told also relates to Captain Nunneley's time at the house. Several guests, including Mrs Playfair Hannay, were staying at the house for an annual ball. She had returned from the ball around two o'clock in the morning, accompanied by Captain Nunneley who showed them to their rooms and lit the gas lamps before leaving them. As they prepared for bed, her roommate passed comment that she hoped she was not awakened again by the men shouting outside as they saddled and prepared their horses for riding. Mrs Playfair Hannay found this remark unusual, as she knew there were no stables anywhere near the house. Her companion refused to believe this and was adamant she had heard the horses and men the previous morning.

The following day when they went downstairs for breakfast, they were met by an army Captain, who had also been staying. He keenly asked the young women whether they had heard the commotion outside just after they had gone upstairs the following night. He went on to tell them he had been in the library when they had returned from the ball, and when the clock struck two, he had heard the distinctive sound of men marching outside and orders being shouted, as though there was a changing of the guards, a sound he was no doubt familiar with from his military career. No one else had however heard this, and it was confirmed that there were had not been any guards outside the house.

It seems what the guests at the house had encountered was some form of replaying of past events. While there were no stables at the house at that time, it is almost inconceivable that a property that had played host to distinguished guests such as Mary, Queen of Scots, and King James II did not have somewhere to stable horses. Earlier in the book, *'Queen Mary's House and Those Who Lived In It'*, there is in fact reference to a description of the house from a sale in 1785, and the details include a coach house confirming that there had indeed once been facilities to keep horses at the premises. It is also entirely reasonable to expect that during the turbulent times in which they lived, Queen Mary and King James II would have been accompanied by armed guards, such as those heard by the Captain at the stroke of two.

A final footnote in the book states that soon after the house being passed into the ownership of St Leonards School, Bishop Plumb carried out a full exorcism on the house to rid it of the spirits. Although I have been unable to find any documentation verifying this, it is not necessarily the sort of action that would be publicised, and as it is noted in a book produced by the school, there is no reason to doubt it. I am also unaware of any further documented reports of incidents at the house since, although rumours persist of ongoing activity.

The front of Queen Mary's House, facing South Street

ST LEONARDS HOUSE

Behind Queen Marys House, opposite St. Leonards Chapel, stands a building known as St Leonards House. This was the home of Sir David Brewster while he was Principal of the United College of St Andrews University from 1838 to 1859. Brewster was a scientist, mathematician, astronomer and inventor, best known for his work on optics. He also remained open minded to the idea of ghosts, neither being a believer nor disbeliever. During his time at St Leonards House, he had extensive refurbishment work carried out and it seems this stirred up something that would test his beliefs in the supernatural.

St Leonards House

In the book *'The Home Life of Sir David Brewster'*, written in 1869 by his daughter, Mrs Margaret M. Gordon, she reveals that her father confessed that he was 'afraid of ghosts, though he did not believe in them'. She goes on to reveal that during his time at St Leonards House, the family were constantly disturbed by ghostly happenings. The text reads:

'Living in an old house, haunted, it was said, by the learned shade of George Buchanan, in which certainly the strangest and most unaccountable noises were frequently heard, his footsteps used sometimes to perform the transit from his study to his bedroom in the dead of night in double-quick time ; and in the morning he used to confess that sitting up alone had made him feel quite eerie.'

George Buchanan was a famous Scottish historian and scholar who had supported the Protestant Reformation and had spent time imprisoned at St. Andrews Castle after being accused of heresy, before escaping and spending a period of time exiled in France. When he returned in 1566, he was made Principal of St. Leonards College, a role that would have led him to live in St. Leonards House. Other than it being one of his places of residence, there is no other information that would show why the spirit of George Buchanan would haunt the building.

George Buchanan, engraving by Jacobus Houbraken (1698 – 1780)

Sir Brewster was to have another visitation in the house, one which would see him fleeing in terror. His daughter recalled how he told her that he had distinctly seen the Reverend Charles Lyon, the Episcopal clergyman and a close friend, rising from the floor like a statue. What made this vision even more unusual, was that the Rev. Lyon was still alive. Sir Brewster rushed to see his friend to make sure no misfortune had befallen him, and was relieved to find he was well. There seemed to be no reason for the figure appearing in the house.

THE BYRE THEATRE

Further along South Street, a narrow lane to the left leads you down past some beautiful historic buildings and to the Byre Theatre. The impressive current building bears no resemblance to its humble beginnings when, in 1933, Alexander Paterson, a local playwright and journalist, decided to lease a semi-derelict cow byre from the Council and, with the help of the Hope Park Church theatre group, transformed it into a theatre. Despite its basic beginning and unusual facilities (the history of the theatre tells that the loft changing rooms were accessed via ladder that had been removed from a decommissioned naval ship), it soon became established as a popular entertainment venue, regularly filled to capacity.

Model of the original Byre Theatre

With the outbreak of the Second World War in 1939, Paterson left to fight with the Royal Air Force and in the spring of 1940 the 'St Andrews Repertory Company' was established to handle the running of the theatre. The group employed the services of Charles Marford, a former stage manager at the Old Vic Theatre in London, who split his time between St Andrews and his family home in London. The 1940 season proved to be difficult for the theatre due to the cast members and the potential audiences being called up for active service in the war. Marford returned for the 1941 season, this time accompanied by his wife, Molly. Although they once again encountered difficulties in finding performers and a skilled workforce, they continued to put on regular performances to ensure the survival of the theatre through these bleak years until, in 1945 at the end of the war, Alexander Paterson returned and assumed the role of manager once again.

By the 1960s, the success of the theatre meant it had outgrown the building, and when it was demolished in 1969 to make way for a road-widening project, the opportunity was taken to improve facilities and a new, larger theatre was built a few hundred yards from the original byre, which opened in 1970, still under the leadership of Alexander Paterson.

By the mid-1980s, Paterson once again desired that the theatre be modernised. Instead, the theatre was again demolished and rebuilt at a cost of £5.5 million (a vast difference compared to the £10 rent paid for the original byre!) with the current theatre first opening its doors in 2001. Unfortunately, Alexander Paterson died in 1989, never living to see the far grander building that grew from his vision. In 2013, the theatre sadly went into liquidation, but it was saved through a management agreement between St. Andrews University, Fife Council and Creative Scotland, and once again is hosting performances from around the country.

The Current Byre Theatre

It seems that Charles Marford, more commonly known as Chas, never quite got over his time at the Byre with actors and staff claiming to have stated to feel his presence at the theatre soon after his death in 1955. Although the ghost is said to have only ever been seen once, and then just in shadow form in a room better known as 'the Green Room', those who encountered the earliest incidents and who had known Chas felt sure it was him that had returned, and that belief has remained since. Common incidents attributed to the invisible spook most include a sudden burst of cold air, unexplained noises, items being moved and chairs in the auditorium lowering and lifting during rehearsals, as though an invisible audience member is watching the performance.

In the book *'A Haunting of Ghosts'*, the author, Helen Cook, tells of one tale that has been directly attributed to Chas. During a performance, a tape was required to be played to provide sound effects. At the appropriate point, the 'play' button was pressed and everyone was shocked when, rather than hearing the expected sounds, the theatre was filled with completely unknown music that not even the theatrical members recognised. The tape was immediately stopped and the show proceeded without the effects. Afterwards, when the audience had all left, the tape was checked and was found only to have the correct sound effects recorded, with no trace of any music.

The ghost of Marford was first reported in the original theatre and, after a short period of inactivity, appeared to have moved to the theatre built in 1969. It was noted that the spirit once again became active when a bust of William Shakespeare, that had been in the original theatre, was brought to the new theatre. During the time when the current theatre was being built, this bust went missing and, interestingly, there have been no reports of ghostly activity since. It would therefore appear that the spirit of Charles Marford had been in some way attached to this bust.

ST MARY'S COLLEGE

St Mary's College, the University's School of Divinity, is situated further along South Street, still housed in its original sixteenth century buildings. Although originally planned by Archbishop James Beaton in 1525, it was not until 1539 that the college was officially founded and James Beaton never saw his dream come to fruition, as he died just a few months later in the autumn of 1539. He was succeeded by his nephew, Cardinal David Beaton, who oversaw the construction of the initial college buildings, which incorporated the earlier Chapel of St John, until his assassination in 1546. Successive Archbishops instructed additional buildings to be added, and work continued until the Reformation brought the town into a period of chaos and destruction. Unlike most of the religious buildings in St Andrews associated with the Catholic faith, the college survived the reformation due to the action of Principle Douglas who, along with many of those involved with the college for the previous decade, opted to join the Protestant reformers rather than face their wrath. After the reformation, the college was re-established as the University's Faculty of Christian Studies.

Within the quadrangle of the College stand two important trees, both of which have led to the University being honoured in the Forestry Commission Scotland's top 100 'Heritage Trees of Scotland' for their preservation. The most dominant is a Holm Oak tree, planted around 1740 and with the circumference of the trunk measuring a massive 3.67 meters (12 feet) it is recorded as the biggest in Scotland.

The quad of St Mary's College, dominated by the Oak Tree

The more historically significant is a smaller Hawthorn tree, which is believed to have been planted by Mary, Queen of Scots, in 1536. The Heritage Trees listing states 'Queen Mary's Hawthorn is living proof that trees don't always have to be big to be important'.

The buildings of St Mary's College include the King James library. Built on the site of the medieval College of St John, this University library is the oldest in Scotland. Originally intended to house books bequeathed to the University by Mary, Queen of Scots, along with the Universities own collections, King James the VI and 1st had offered to provide the funding for the library building in 1612, although due to subsequent financial difficulties, the construction was not completed until 1643. The outbreak of the plague in Edinburgh in 1645 saw the building taking a position of elevated importance with the Scottish Parliament temporarily moving to St Andrews and meeting in the lower hall of the library. During this time, Sir Robert Spottiswoode, a prominent judge and politician, was tried for treason in the hall. Despite being the son of John Spottiswoode, the Archbishop of St Andrews, and holding the position of Lord President of the Court of Session, the head of the judiciary in Scotland, Robert Spottiswoode was a deeply unpopular man. He had allied with King Charles I in his actions against the covenanters, an action that eventually forced him to resign his post in the Court of Session and flee to England, where he remained under the protection of King Charles until he was captured at the Battle of Philiphaugh, which took place near the town of Selkirk in the Scottish Borders between the Royalists and the Covenanters on 13th September 1645. After being transferred to St. Andrews, he was charged with acting against the State and, despite pleading his innocence, he was convicted to death and beheaded at the town's Market Cross. The University then submitted a petition to Parliament asking that Spottiswoode's vast collection of books be gifted to the library on the basis that both he and his father had borrowed them from the University, but did wrong by not returning them, effectively accusing them of theft. The Parliament found in favour of the University, and ordered that all the books be handed over to the library. The short term use by the Scottish Parliament has had a long lasting effect of the hall, with it becoming known as Parliament Hall and remaining to be used as a debating chamber for the University Debating Society to this day.

Another significant feature of the library originates through the studies of the astronomer and scientist, James Gregory, who based his laboratory in the library building. Despite suffering a stroke at the age of just 36, which led to his death a few days later, Gregory achieved much in his short life. He became the Professor of Mathematics at St. Andrews University at the age of 30, and invented the Gregorian Telescope, a design for a reflecting telescope which pre-dates Sir Isaac Newton's Newtonian telescope (widely considered to be the first reflecting telescope) by five years. Gregory also laid a Meridian line across his laboratory, which, in October 2014 was widely covered in the news when the University staked a claim that St. Andrews is 'the place where time began', with the Gregory's Meridian line pre-dating the Greenwich Meridian line by two hundred years. To mark the significance of Gregory's work, a brass line and plaque have been laid in the pavement outside the library to mark his Meridian line.

The Gregorian Meridian Line

The library was home to a particularly gruesome artefact for several centuries, known only as the Suicide Skeleton. In 1707, one of the University's messengers hung themselves in St Mary's College. Suicide was deemed to be a sin at the time and so, rather than being buried, the body was sent to Dundee University to be used by medical students. The skeleton was articulated, and returned to St. Andrews where it was displayed in the library until, in 1941, it was finally given a proper burial.

The existence of the skeleton led to many tales of strange happenings and ghostly sightings among the student population, although with no records of hauntings that can be directly attributed to the skeleton, it can only be stated that there was an assumption that the spirit of the messenger was responsible for these encounters.

A ghost story was written about the King James Library by Margaret Oliphant (1828 – 1897) titled *'The Library Window'*, in which she tells of a young lady visiting her aunt in St. Andrews. While sitting in a window seat reading, she starts to see a young man in the window of the library on the opposite side of the road, but as the library window had been built over several years prior with only a false window remaining, she realises this cannot be so. As she continues to sit and read over the coming days, the figure of the man also continues to appear with increasing detail, allowing her to see that he is seated at a desk, constantly writing. She told her aunt about the man she saw, who insisted that it is impossible to see inside the building through the false windows and so she must be imagining it. The sightings however persisted, until the truth was eventually revealed. The window was indeed false, but the young man was a ghost, considered to be a curse on the women of the family. The story told that many years ago, prior to the library windows being built over, one of the young woman's ancestors had been seated in the window seat of the house, just as she had when she first saw the figure. She had glanced across and noticed the man sat at the window of the library opposite, working at his desk. He looked up and their eyes met, prompting the girl to wave at him in a flirtatious manner. Unfortunately, the girl's brothers witnessed this and, mistakenly thinking the man had responded, her brothers dragged him outside and beat him so savagely that he died. Ever since, his ghost has appeared to successive generations of women in the family.

Although this story is widely considered to be a work of fiction, between 1765 and 1767, there was so much demand on space in the library that the walls were raised, and a gallery added with the upper floor windows facing South Street being blocked with bookcases, and so it is true that some of the windows are now false. The story is also told in a leaflet produced by the University providing information on the library, all of which may suggest there is more to the story than initially appears.

BAKERS LANE AND PONTIUS PILATE

Opposite the King James Library, there is a narrow lane that leads to Market Street, named Bakers Lane. Although little known today, a curious discovery on a building in this lane led to a lot of speculation at the time. While carrying out repair work to the roughcasting on one of the properties in 1895, workmen were surprised to discover that a bulge in the roughcasting was not in fact due to any fault, but instead was covering a hideous stone carved face. Described as being a crowned, angry face with fanged teeth, long hair and whiskers, the house on which it was found had once belonged to the Knights Templars, leading to the belief that the face represented Pontius Pilate, the Roman Governor who oversaw the trial of Jesus Christ and sentenced him to death by crucifixion.

A newspaper article from May 1939 reports that the house had been demolished but the face saved, with the town council deciding to ask a Mr T. T. Fordyce for permission for the face to be fitted to the gable of his property that faced Bakers Lane. The face remains on this spot today, although it has sadly lacked any attempts at preservation and the features are now indistinguishable.

The face of Pontius Pilate

I was provided a personal story regarding the face of Pontius Pilate by a local lady named Mary. She informed me that when her grandfather was a child, he used to live with his parents in the property on which the face was first discovered. Mary's grandfather, who she described as not a man who would make things up, told how he became scared of his bedroom, as his bed had started to move across the room and sometimes even lift off the floor and drop back down. This classic poltergeist activity would seem to have commenced around the time that the face of Pilate was exposed, and so perhaps there was good reason why it had been covered in the past. Since the face was moved and the building demolished, there have not been any further reports of incidents that I am aware of.

The entrance to Barkers Lane

BLACKFRIARS CHAPEL

Madras College, the town's well known high school, is situated towards the west end of South Street. Dating back to 1833, the school takes its name from its founder, Rev Dr Andrew Bell who, while acting as the chaplain to the regiments of the East India Company in Madras, devised a new teaching method to provide a full education to the children of the soldiers, despite the lack of teachers. Upon his return to Scotland, Bell set about encouraging schools to adopt his method of education, known as 'the Madras system', and at the time of his death in 1832, over 10,000 schools were using it.

In front of the school stands the remains of a medieval church of the Dominican Friars, better known as the Blackfriars due to the colour of their robes, leading to the building being commonly known as Blackfriars Chapel. Despite the building dating back to the sixteenth century, there is relatively little history surrounding it, due to its short life-span. Construction of the chapel was completed in 1510 and it housed five friars. By 1559, St Andrews was in the midst of the Protestant Reformation, and the chapel was one of the first buildings targeted by the reformers, who violently banished the friars and destroyed the chapel.

The remains of Blackfriars Chapel

The ghost of one of the friars has been seen walking at the remains of the chapel, as though continuing to carry out his day to day duties. This phantom is believed to be that of Alexander Campbell, who was a key figure in the trial and execution of the Protestant Reformer Patrick Hamilton (who will be discussed later) in 1528. According to the book *The British Cyclopedia of Literature, History, Geography, Law and Politics* by Charles F. Partington, published in 1846, Campbell had insulted Hamilton while he was awaiting execution, publically objecting to his treachery and condemning him to answer for his part in the reformation and to face the judgement of Christ.

A few days later, Campbell was struck down by an unidentified illness from which he never recovered, and he died shortly after. An alternative version of events states that during the burning of Patrick Hamilton, Campbell was badly burned himself and died from his injuries. The local belief is that this was the will of Christ, casting judgement on Campbell for his actions rather than on Hamilton, and that his spirit was condemned to forever remain at the chapel.

Blackfriars Chapel viewed from the rear

GREYFRIARS CHAPEL AND GARDEN

Directly opposite Blackfriars Chapel, Bell Street (named after Andrew Bell) leads up to a crossroads with Market Street. The street opposite Bell Street was originally called North Bell Street but was later renamed Greyfriars Garden, as the road passes through the garden ground of the former Greyfriars Chapel. Established by Bishop James Kennedy in 1458, the Franciscan Friary known as Greyfriars, again due to the colour of the robes worn by the Friars, predates Blackfriars by around fifty years. The complex comprised of a church, a cloistered courtyard and a cemetery. The Friary is believed to have originally housed around twenty four friars, although by the time of the reformation this had decreased to around six. As with Blackfriars Chapel, at the start of the Reformation the friars were forcibly removed and the chapel was destroyed. Today nothing exists of any of the buildings, with the Students Union now built on the site of the church, and the buildings forming the surrounding streets being built on the friary's garden grounds and orchards. The only part of the complex that remains is a well that is situated in the garden of one of the properties in Greyfriars Garden.

The Well in Greyfriars Garden

W. T. Linskill tells of a tale connected with the chapel in his 1911 book *'St. Andrews Ghost Stories'*. In the story, he recalled meeting with an old friend named Allan Beauchamp while he was travelling in the Highlands of Scotland. The two men sat talking and inevitably, the conversation turned to ghosts, at which point Beauchamp suddenly remarked that it is curious for a man to be pursued by a grinning skull. Linskill initially dismissed such a suggestion, but his companion was insistent that he himself had been followed by a skull for several years and eventually agreed to tell Linskill his story.

He revealed that around 1513, one of his relatives, Neville de Beauchamp, lived in Scotland and married a woman from Perth. Neville had been a hard drinker and gambler, and his wife had died just a few years after the wedding, leading those who knew them to believe she had died from a broken heart over the way her husband treated her. Full of remorse, Neville fled to St Andrews and to Greyfriars Friary, where he became a man of god. His wife's relatives were not so forgiving, and pursued him intent on avenging her death. They traced Neville to Greyfriars and, after forcing their way into the church, her brother beheaded Neville with a single swipe of his sword as he stood in the aisle. He could only watch in horror as, while the body fell to the ground, the head remained floating before letting out an ear piercing scream and flying up to the roof of the church where it disappeared.

Neville's body was buried, but the head was never recovered. Over the coming years, the head started to appear at seemingly random times, floating above the monastery, always screaming. The head seemed to decompose, just as the rest of the body would have, until all that remained was the skull. At this point it stopped appearing at the monastery, but instead began to appear to members of the Beauchamp family.

Linskill was keen to hear more, and Beauchamp explained that a few years earlier, while staying in St. Andrews, he received notification that his uncle had died abroad. Although he had never met his uncle, he knew of tales that he had been tormented by the screaming skull that appeared to him at odd times in unexpected places. Conscious of the fact that he was now the last surviving member of the Beauchamp family, his thoughts had quickly turned to whether he would now be the focus of the skulls attention. He was to receive his answer shortly after when, on a stormy evening, he felt an uncontrollable desire to go out for a walk through the town. In the dark streets, he felt as though he was going into some form of a trance and not in control of which direction he took. He soon found himself turning into North Bell Street (as it was still known then) but rather than the road and houses he was familiar with, several buildings that he did not recognise stood before him. He walked forward and entered one, only to find himself standing in a chapel. In front of him, he could see a friar being confronted by a group of angry men, and could only stand and watch as one of the men raised his sword and beheaded the friar. The shock of realising that he had just witnessed the murder of his ancestor, which had happened centuries before, brought him back to his senses. Feeling the rain on his skin, he looked around and saw that he was sitting on the wall of the school, which is also on the site of the former chapel, surrounded by the buildings he knew. With his clothes soaked through, he stood to walk home and noticed a small, white object on the ground at his feet. From the round shape he assumed it was a ball and, frustrated at the events of the night, he swung his foot to kick it away in an attempt to relieve some of his tension. Despite the force of his kick, the ball merely rolled over, revealing it was in fact a skull. With its empty eye sockets staring up at him, the skull appeared to smile, before gnashing its teeth at him and shooting up into the night sky, screaming as it did so.

The skull had continued to haunt him since, with him never knowing where or when it would appear. Linskill reported that after the meeting, he received correspondence from his friend on a regular basis giving details of the skulls visitations. He revealed that he had eventually managed to contain the skull in a casket where it remained mostly quiet, only occasionally moaning and screaming. He did however advise that the skull disappears from the casket twice a year for two days, and he has no idea where it goes during that time. He suggested to Linskill that it was possible it was returning to haunt the chapel on the date of the murder, and he asked Linskill to let him know if there were any reports of the skull being seen in St. Andrews, which would allow him to test this theory.

Given Linskill's apparent tendency to use artistic licence to the maximum in his story telling, it is fair to assume that this tale has been considerably exaggerated. With no historical records that would seem to support the incidents that are said to have led to the cursed skull, this is another story that can only be classed as local ghost-lore that has been passed down. Interestingly, although there are no further tales of sightings of the skull that I am aware of, there have been reports of a headless monk walking the grounds of the former chapel, and perhaps this is the spirit of Beauchamp still seeking his long lost head.

Details of another phantom monk connected to Greyfriars are given by Helen Cook in her book *'A Haunting of Ghosts'*, in which she tells of the figure of a Franciscan Friar. Those who have witnessed the spirit report that while in the area around the former chapel, the figure of the friar suddenly materialised in front of them. Few felt scared by this unexplained occurrence, as to see the Friar is considered to bring you good luck.

In March 2012, road-resurfacing work at Greyfriars Garden was called to a halt when human skeletons were discovered just a few inches below the surface. Archaeological investigations suggest that these were bodies from the cemetery of Greyfriars Chapel, and the bones were likely to date back to between 1458 and 1559. It is therefore highly likely that the bodies of more monks were disturbed during the construction of the buildings in the area, which may offer an explanation for the phantom figures that have since been seen.

Skeleton found at Greyfriars Garden (photo supplied by Fife Council Archaeology Department)

ST ANDREWS CINEMA HOUSE

Continuing along North Street, you will pass a block of housing that looks quite out of place with the rest of the area. This was the site of the Cinema House, St Andrews first purpose built movie theatre. Originally designed to only show silent films with a live orchestra playing, the Cinema House first opened its doors in 1919. Sound systems were installed in 1929 to keep up with the development of movies, and in 1934, the opening of the New Picture House, just a short distance away on the opposite side of North Street, brought the first real competition to the Cinema House. Despite this, it continued to thrive until December 1979 when, with little notice, it closed following the retirement of Jack Humphries, who had been the manager for fifty one years. The building quickly fell into a state of disrepair and was demolished in 1980 to make way for the new flats.

The flats occupying the site of the former Cinema House

As a child, I used to regularly visit the Cinema House to watch whatever new blockbuster had been released. The cinema always seemed to have an old fashioned feel, perhaps an odd comment to make about the building given that it was fairly old, but I always felt something in the atmosphere that I more related to much older properties. The cinema was said to be haunted, with the belief that this ghost was a former member of staff. The most common report was that one of the seats in the upper gallery would move, as though someone was sitting there. The seats were all fitted with springs so that when not in use they would fold up, yet the seat in question would often be noted to be lowered, something that could only be achieved by applying weight to the seat, such as when someone sat on them. The sound of footsteps were also a regular occurrence, particularly after all of the public had left. The staff would report that while in the ticket booth that was at the bottom of one of the flights of stairs, they would hear someone walking down but no one ever emerged at the bottom of the steps. Whenever the stairs and gallery were checked, there was never anyone there.

Sadly, with the loss of the Cinema House, the chance of gaining further evidence of the reported strange happenings has also been lost. Although many cinemas are reported to be haunted, I can personally vouch that the Cinema House had the right atmosphere to support the claims.

ST SALVATOR'S TOWER AND PATRICK HAMILTON

Across the street from the site of the Cinema House, the Chapel of St Salvator, or more precisely the distinctive clock tower, can be seen for miles. The chapel was founded in 1450 as part of Bishop Kennedy's College of the Holy Saviour, and it remains an important piece of gothic architecture. That said, it is a shadow of the original building as, along with most other places of religion in the town, it suffered at the hands of the Protestant Reformers who destroyed all of the statues that once stood in the many canopied niches around the exterior. The tomb of Bishop Kennedy, which is inside the chapel, was also damaged, and the stained glass windows smashed. The chapel continued to stand empty and decaying for almost a century and would have been lost had it not been for the actions of Provost Skene who, in 1680, managed to raise substantial funds for the sympathetic restoration of the building. In the 1760s a far less sympathetic act of 'restoration' was carried out when the original stone roof of the chapel was deliberately collapsed, creating a crash that was said to have shaken the whole town, before being replaced with the

St Salvator's Tower

slate roof we see today. Several other attempts at restoration were carried out over the next century, mostly being the designer's interpretation of how the original features may have looked rather than an actual replica.

Passing through the archway at the base of the clock tower, you will enter the quadrangle of St Salvator's college, where you will find yourself surrounded by grand looking buildings with striking architectural features. As with the Chapel, all is however not as it appears, and these seemingly ancient buildings date back only to the mid-1800s. A description of the original buildings is given in the *Handbook to St. Andrews*, by D. May Fleming, first published in 1881 in which he says:

'all the old classrooms, judging from sketches and photographs, were very plain buildings, with square-headed windows, and no relieving architectural feature save perhaps the long arched-corridors'.

Perhaps the most interesting quote provided by Fleming regarding the earlier buildings on the site is from Dr J. W. Taylor, who in the 1830's described them as being:

'Dingy and decaying and old world like it seemed, but it was full of interest. On its east and south sides were the ruins of the houses in which the College bread was baked, and the College beer brewed. Along the north side extended a range of barrack-like buildings, supplying in its upper stories rooms for the collegians, and from which the last occupant was driven by the nightly invasion of a ghost'.

Unfortunately, he does not go any further into detail of this ghost that terrified the students so much that they refused to stay, although an article published in the *Dundee Courier* newspaper on 22nd April 1904 revealed that it was the ghost of a deceased university professor that had haunted the buildings. No reason is offered as to why the spirit of the professor had remained there.

Returning through the archway and back onto North Street, you will see the letters 'PH' in the cobbles. This marks the sport where Protestant Reformer, Patrick Hamilton, was burned to death in such a horrific way that it has forever left its mark on St. Andrews. Born in Scotland, Hamilton travelled around Europe where he met some of the fathers of the European Reformation such as Martin Luther and, when he returned to Scotland, he was keen to relay his new knowledge. He took a place at St Leonard's College in St. Andrews where he began preaching and began to build himself a following among the students at the college. With Scotland still being a Catholic country, it was not long until his preaching came to the attention of Dr. James Beaton, the Archbishop of St. Andrews who, keen to crush any potential uprising, ordered that Hamilton be arrested and tried for heresy. Hamilton was warned and he fled to Germany, but only stayed there a few months before returning to Scotland, seemingly accepting that if his fate was to face death for his beliefs, that was preferable to living a life in hiding.

Beaton invited Hamilton to St. Andrews stating that he wished to discuss his beliefs, but it was a trap, and he was seized during the night at St. Andrews Castle. On 29th February 1528, just hours after being tried and convicted of heresy, Hamilton was bound to a stake with iron chains in front of the Chapel of St. Salvators. Only a small pile of coal and wood had been stacked below him, yet due to his refusal to deny his Protestant beliefs, he was to be burned alive. He was just twenty four years old. A small amount of gunpowder was poured into the kindling below him in an attempt to enhance the fire, and a trail laid to a safe distance, before it was lit. The powder beneath him ignited, but there had not been enough kindling it was blown out of the woodpile in the explosion, which also badly burned Hamilton's hands and face. The fire had failed to light and so the process was repeated, but again the explosion only resulted in causing more burns to Hamilton. Realising they had run out of gunpowder, Hamilton was left chained in agony from his injuries while fresh supplies of powder were brought from the castle. It was during this time that Friar Alexander Campbell of the Blackfriars verbally assaulted him and condemned him to face the judgement of Christ.

After a third attempt, the wood eventually started to burn, but only slowly. When the fire continued to burn without any ferocity, the wood was checked and was found to be wet. The speed of Hamilton's trial and execution had left insufficient time to properly prepare the fire, resulting in the wood that had not being properly dried being used. No doubt aggravated at how these failures would be seen by the gathered townsfolk, orders were issued for dry wood to be gathered, again probably from the castle, and this was thrown into the flames.

Eventually, six hours after his ordeal had started, the flames gathered sufficient strength to take Hamilton's life. Just before he died, he is said to have cried 'how long, O Lord, shall darkness overwhelm this realm? How long wilt thou suffer this tyranny of men? Lord Jesus, receive my spirit'.

The prolonged agony endured by Hamilton is believed to have created energy so strong that when his spirit left his body, it burned the image of his face into the stonework of St. Salvator's clock tower. The face remains visible today on the fifth row of stones above the Coat of Arms.

Patrick Hamilton's Face

There is a local superstition among the students of the town surrounding the spot where Hamilton died. Visitors will generally observe the students walking around the letters rather than over them, as most do. This is due to there being a belief that to walk over the letters 'P.H.' will

bring them bad luck and cause them to fail their exams and for that reason, they are avoided.

The letters P.H. marking the spot where Patrick Hamilton died

SUPERNATURAL St ANDREWS

THE GHOSTS OF MARY, QUEEN OF SCOTS

There are a number of spirits in the town associated with Mary, probably the most famous of Scottish Queens. In her book, *A Haunting of Ghosts*, Helen Cook gives brief details of some ghosts from the town centre. She advises that the spirit of James, Earl of Bothwell, has been seen as a young man in the town. As he is identified as the third husband of Mary, Queen of Scots, we can determine this is the ghost of the 4th Earl of Bothwell, James Hepburn.

Born around 1536, Hepburn attained the titles of Earl of Bothwell and Lord High Admiral of Scotland when his father died in 1556. Despite being Protestant and the Scottish Royals being Catholic, he supported Mary of Guise, the mother of Mary, Queen of Scots, who had been appointed to administer the state while the queen was an infant. He was given Hermitage Castle in the Scottish Borders and appointed Lieutenant of the Border for his loyalty. In 1560, he travelled to Copenhagen, the capital city of Denmark, where he met a young lady named Anna Thorndsen, the daughter of a Danish Admiral. They were soon engaged to be married, with a large sum of money to be paid by the bride's parents to the happy couple. There are conflicting versions whether the marriage ever took place, but it is known that Hepburn deserted Anna, and took the money. After the death of Mary of Guise, Mary, Queen of Scots, returned to Scotland and following the death of her first husband in France, Hepburn also returned and became one of the Queen's main advisors.

Unfortunately for Hepburn, the young queen had other advisors, all seeking to influence her for their own good and opposing him. As a result, he faced endless allegations being made against him, resulting in him spending time in the prisons of Edinburgh Castle before being exiled to England, where he spent a short time in the Tower of London. Several attempts to murder him had also been made and, facing financial disaster and constant danger, he eventually fled to France.

In 1565, he returned to Scotland. By this time, the Queen had married her cousin, Lord Darnley, a marriage that was opposed by many of the nobles in Scotland. Seeing an opportunity to win the favour of the queen, Hepburn stepped in and helped to quell any uprisings against the marriage. After a short period of peace, Lord Darnley became unhappy with his own position in the marriage as the husband to the Queen, and he sought to become her equal, and the King of Scotland. Mary initially accepted his demands, but soon the marriage became strained and she revoked his status as king. Mary had become close to her private secretary, David Rizzio, during the turmoil of her marriage, and her enemies seized on this and Darnley's discontent, by suggesting that Rizzio was to blame for their unhappiness, in the hope that would bring down the queen.

On 9th March 1566, Rizzio was pulled away from a supper held by the queen and violently murdered in front of her by a gang led by Darnley. A gun was pointed at the Queen, who was heavily pregnant, to stop her intervening. Realising her own life was in danger, Mary managed to talk to her husband, who although present had not played an active part in the murder, and she was able to once again convince him to support her and to oppose those who carried out the dreadful deed. Knowing they had to escape Edinburgh, it was Hepburn who once again stepped forward to assist, by managing to arrange their escape from the city and providing safe accommodation for them at Dunbar Castle. On the 18th March, Mary returned to Edinburgh, accompanied by an army of around five thousand men provided by Hepburn. Upon seeing the forces enter the city, her enemies who had plotted against her and killed Rizzio offered no resistance and fled.

The Queen's marriage continued to struggle, with Lord Darnley becoming increasingly remote from his wife, even after the birth of their son, James, who would eventually become King James VI of Scotland and I of England, the first King of Great Britain. Hepburn and the Queen meanwhile grew closer, with rumours that they had become romantically involved with each other. In the early hours of the morning of 10th February 1567, an explosion rocked Edinburgh and it was soon discovered that the house in which Darnley had been staying had been completely destroyed. The basement had been filled with gunpowder, which had been ignited. Darnley's body was found in the gardens at the rear, along with the body of one of his servants. There were signs that Darnley had been strangled, and it was believed that the explosion had been an attempt to take his life, but he had escaped with his servant moments before, only to be captured and strangled. The finger of blame was pointed squarely at Hepburn, and he stood trial for the killings. The trial ended up being little more than a show, put on to appease his accusers, and he was quickly acquitted. In April 1567, he asked the Queen to marry him (despite still being married himself) but she turned him down. He is then said to have kidnapped her and raped her, after which she agreed to become his wife. This would seem quite unimaginable today, however, there is a suggestion the kidnapping was an elaborate ploy with the queen being a willing participant, and the subsequent story of her being raped was to cover the fact she was already pregnant with Hepburn's child. He promptly arranged a divorce with his own wife, Jean Gordon, on the basis that he had an affair with one of their servants and, on 15th May 1567, he married the Queen.

This marriage was even less popular than her marriage to Darnley, and the couple were forced to flee to Dunbar Castle. They gathered an army to try to defeat the nobles that opposed them and, on 15th June 1567 at Cranberry Hill, their forces met. Realising that the army brought by the nobles was far larger than their own, and they faced certain defeat, Mary offered to surrender herself on the basis that Hepburn was given safe passage into exile. With the queen being the main target, the offer was accepted and she was taken back to Edinburgh before being imprisoned at Loch Leven Castle, which marked the start of nineteen years in captivity and where it transpired she was pregnant to Darnley, as suspected, but sadly she miscarried her twin babies. Hepburn tried to gather support to free the Queen, but due to his unpopularity he failed, and subsequently had no option but to set sail for Norway, where he believed he would be safe.

This would turn out to be the biggest mistake of his life as he was intercepted by the relatives of Anna Thorndsen while passing through Danish controlled waters. He was charged with abandonment and ordered to repay the dowry that he had taken, something that he was in no financial position to do. He was sent to the notorious Dragsholm Castle in Zealand, Denmark, where he was chained to a stone pillar and left in solitary confinement. Ten years later, he died, having been driven completely insane and worn a groove in the floor beneath him from walking round the pillar. A groove was also said to have been worn in the pillar from the chain being pulled repeatedly round as he walked. Legend has it that Anna was not finished with her revenge, and had his mummified body dug up and placed on display at the castle, where it remained until the mid-1900s when it was buried in a crypt at a nearby church.

Although the tale of Hepburn's turbulent life has all of the ingredients for a good ghost story (his ghost is in fact said to haunt Dragsholm Castle, where he suffered so badly and lost his mind and life) some would ask why he would also haunt St. Andrews. A possible explanation could lie in the actions he took during his life. It is known that Mary had grown to hate her second Husband, Lord Darnley, due to how easily he was influenced to assist in the murder of David Rizzio and to plot against her, and it is widely accepted that it was Hepburn who was responsible for his murder. This action required Hepburn to take great personal risk, as he had done in the past, to save the queen. Hepburn was also willing to use a story of kidnap and rape, which would severely tarnish his own character, but cover the queen's affair and pregnancy and again save her honour. And as they faced their final battle together, it was the queen who was willing to sacrifice herself to allow Darnley to go free. If all of this is true, it is apparent that the couple were deeply and truly in love with each other. As mentioned earlier in the book, it is known Queen Mary spent time in St. Andrews, and Hepburn is believed to have stayed at the castle on several occasions. It is highly probable that they would have met during this enjoyable, far less troublesome, time of their lives, and this is perhaps where Darnley first fell in love with the queen. With ghosts often reported to return to places of significance and with happy memories, it would not seem unreasonable for the younger shade of Hepburn to return to St Andrews.

Another ghost in the town associated with Queen Mary is that of a headless man seen in Market Street. This is believed to be Pierre de Bocosel de Chastelard, a French poet who's love for the Queen would have fatal consequences. He had spent time with Mary while she was in France and after the death of her first husband, he had written poems for her to try to console her. He then visited her in Scotland but his love had turned into an obsession and he was caught in Edinburgh hiding in the Queen's bedchamber. Mary excused him for this, but he did not learn from this as, after travelling with the Royal party to Burntisland in Fife, he was again caught hiding in her chamber at Rossend Castle. This time the Queen demanded that he be killed on the spot, but instead he was taken to St. Andrews where he was executed at the Market Cross, with his last words, directed towards Queen Mary who was watching, being 'Adieu, loveliest and most cruel of princesses'.

Off course, the ghost of Queen Mary is said to have been seen in the town as well, at various locations, although bearing in mind almost every historic town and place in Scotland lays claim to sightings of the phantom queen, I mention this solely for completeness.

Mary in Captivity, by Nicholas Hilliard, Circa 1578

THE McINTOSH HALL

The student forums tell of many stories of strange happenings in the numerous residences in the town. Ranging from the small guest houses to the large university owned accommodation blocks, most seem to have at least one room or corridor with cold spots, eerie feelings or unexplained noises. One of the most talked about is the McIntosh Hall in Abbotsford Crescent. Those walking on Abbotsford Crescent could easily feel they had been transported to old Edinburgh, which is no doubt due to the much respected Edinburgh architect, John Chesser, who was described as 'the prime exponent of terrace design at the time', overseeing their construction.

The McIntosh Halls

The buildings date back to 1865 and comprised of a number of private houses and a hotel, all of which were purchased by the University and converted into a hall of residence. The hotel, named the Chattan Hotel and bought in 1921, resulted in the residences being better known as the Chattan, a name still used today.

Reports of the incidents include cold areas that never seem to heat up, no matter how hot the rest of the building is, and footsteps being heard running down a corridor, continuing along the original corridor even though this was been altered during renovation work and no longer exists. There are also reports of lights being seen switching on and off in a section of the building that had been closed off. One particularly unpleasant report was made by two students, who both stayed in the same part of the building but at different times. They both reported experiencing an unpleasant feeling in their room, seeing a dark figure walking through the room and occasionally awakening to find the figure standing beside their bed, staring down at them though he had no distinguishable features. One had asked for prayers to be said in the room to cleanse it, after which they reported things quietened down, although the cleaner would still complain that the room was notably colder than the others. The man called in to say the prayers reportedly said that he sensed it was not an evil spirit, but one that seemed to not know that he was dead, probably due to dying suddenly, resulting in the spirit being confused as to why others were staying in his room.

Researching the records, there was a newspaper report in the *Daily Record* on 30th October 1916, which tells that a gentleman who lived in one of the private residences at Abbotsford Crescent had died suddenly after a cycling accident. He had been travelling from St. Andrews to nearby Guardbridge the previous Friday when his bike was involved in a collision with a lorry and a horse. He had insisted he was fine after the accident, and continued on his way, but it seems he collapsed soon after as a result of his injuries. His body was not found until the next day, when efforts to resuscitate him were unsuccessful. Perhaps this is who still walks the rooms of his former home.

The most commonly seen figure appears to be that of an elderly looking. There are conflicting stories surrounding the background to this spectre. Some say she owned a house in the terrace and refused to sell it to the University, which prevented them from joining up all of the buildings internally. When she died, the University managed to buy it resulting in her angry spirit remaining, still unhappy that the University managed to get the house in the end. The alternate story is that she left the house to the University in her will, but loved the house so much that she has never left it. Whatever the correct story is, she is always seen in the same area of the halls, an area that was once a mid-terraced house.

OTHER TOWN CENTRE TALES

There are numerous other tales of hauntings within the town centre that have either come from personal stories told to me or are those that are more difficult to document, hence I can only provide brief details. I recently visited an old house on North Street, close to the cathedral, which had been beautifully renovated by the owner. As work such as this can sometimes disturb things from the past, I enquired if they had ever experienced anything unusual in the house and was informed that a young girl had recently been seen on the stairs. Visitors also had a general feeling that the first floor landing was cold and one guest, who had psychic abilities, began to ask about the spirit of the child that played on the stairs. They were able to assure the home owners that she was a good ghost and would cause no harm, although the identity of the girl or why she is still there remains a mystery.

The Edinburgh Woollen Mill on Market Street is popular with both locals and visitors, however, according to the student discussion forum 'The Sinner', those who have worked there had found the first floor stock room to be an uncomfortable and creepy place to be, with one forum user reporting that while they were looking for an item for a customer in the stock room, they felt something brush past them. Knowing they were alone, they had felt unnerved but convinced themselves it was probably just a draft. They then felt someone tap them on the shoulder, at which point they fled.

Another user on the same forum reported strange goings on in the former Woolworths store, further along Market Street. They claimed that shopping trollies would be seem moving around the store, unaided, on a regular basis, and that stock would constantly fall off the shelves when the store was closed, even though the shelves were fitted with a plastic frontage meaning items would need to be physically lifted up and over before falling. In addition, it was reported that a light would frequently switch on overnight, though curiously it was never the same light, excluding the likelihood of an electrical fault in one of the fittings.

There have also been strange goings on at a building site close to Blackfriars Chapel. The contractor advised me that materials and tools have been going missing overnight only to be found in another area later that day, or being found where they had been left, but several days later. This is typical poltergeist activity that can be caused by things long laid to rest being disturbed during building work.

On 19th November 1936, *The Dundee Courier and Advertiser* published a story told by Professor Rose of St. Andrews University. He described what he considered to have been a ghostly encounter he had experienced at his house in the town. He explained that one night he had awoken with a horrible feeling that he was not alone. He had been paralysed with fear for a short time before lighting a candle and checking around the room. Having found nothing untoward, he returned to bed and managed to fall asleep, but soon he awoke again with the same feeling. He again lit the candle and checked the room but found nothing. Eventually he managed to get back to sleep. When he awoke in the morning he recalled the events of the night before and reached for his candle to light it, only to discover there were no candles anywhere in the room. He was unable to offer any explanation as to who, or what, had removed the candles.

A pedlar (a traveling salesman) who was murdered in a cellar in South Street is mentioned by both Helen Cook and W.T. Linskill in their books. Details are somewhat scarce, although Linskill states that he brushes his ice cold hand down the cheeks of anyone who dares to enter his basement. Unfortunately with such limited details, it is difficult to find more facts. There are certainly many reports in the newspaper archives of pedlars in St. Andrews, including on South Street, being involved in various crimes or misdemeanours, but I have not been able to find details of one being murdered, although that doesn't mean it didn't happen, it only indicates that the murder was not reported or investigated.

Archbishop Sharp's phantom coach has also reportedly been seen travelling along South Street in the early morning on the anniversary of his murder. As with the sightings in the Pends, the only sound is said to come from the wheels of the coach rumbling over the old cobbled streets that once lay there. The horses are completely silent with not a sound from their hooves or harnesses.

There is also another account of the sighting of the ghost of John Knox in the town centre, as told in the 2009 book, *The Lore of Scotland*, by Jennifer Westwood and Sophia Kingshill. The incident is said to have taken place in the late nineteenth century when a university lecturer had spent a Sunday evening at a friend's house. He left for home in the early hours of the morning, but returned shortly afterwards, shocked and terrified by what he had witnessed.

The lecturer told that he had walked as far as St Katherine's School (now the Universities Barron Theatre) in North Street when he suddenly noticed a very stern looking man approaching him. He had not encountered anyone else during his short walk and there was no-one else in sight, and so he was quite concerned by the unfriendly appearance of this man, who seemed to be wearing some religious clothing in the form of a long gown with ministerial bands on show. A long, grey beard was noticeable from below the hood. As he watched, he noticed another man walking a short distance behind, wearing some pieces of armour. As the figures came closer, the lecturer was drawn to the minister's eyes, which he described as being 'cold and penetrating'. They passed, silently and without interaction, and it was while they did so that the lecturer had a proper look at the minister's face and, noticing the distinctive features, he immediately recognised the man as John Knox.

The book goes on to tell that Andrew Laing (1844-1912), a local folklorist who lived in the town, had looked into the story in more detail, particularly regarding the curious second figure. In the records that he studied, he found a note stating that during the reformation years, a City Guard was appointed to follow Knox to provide protection.

FURTHER AFIELD

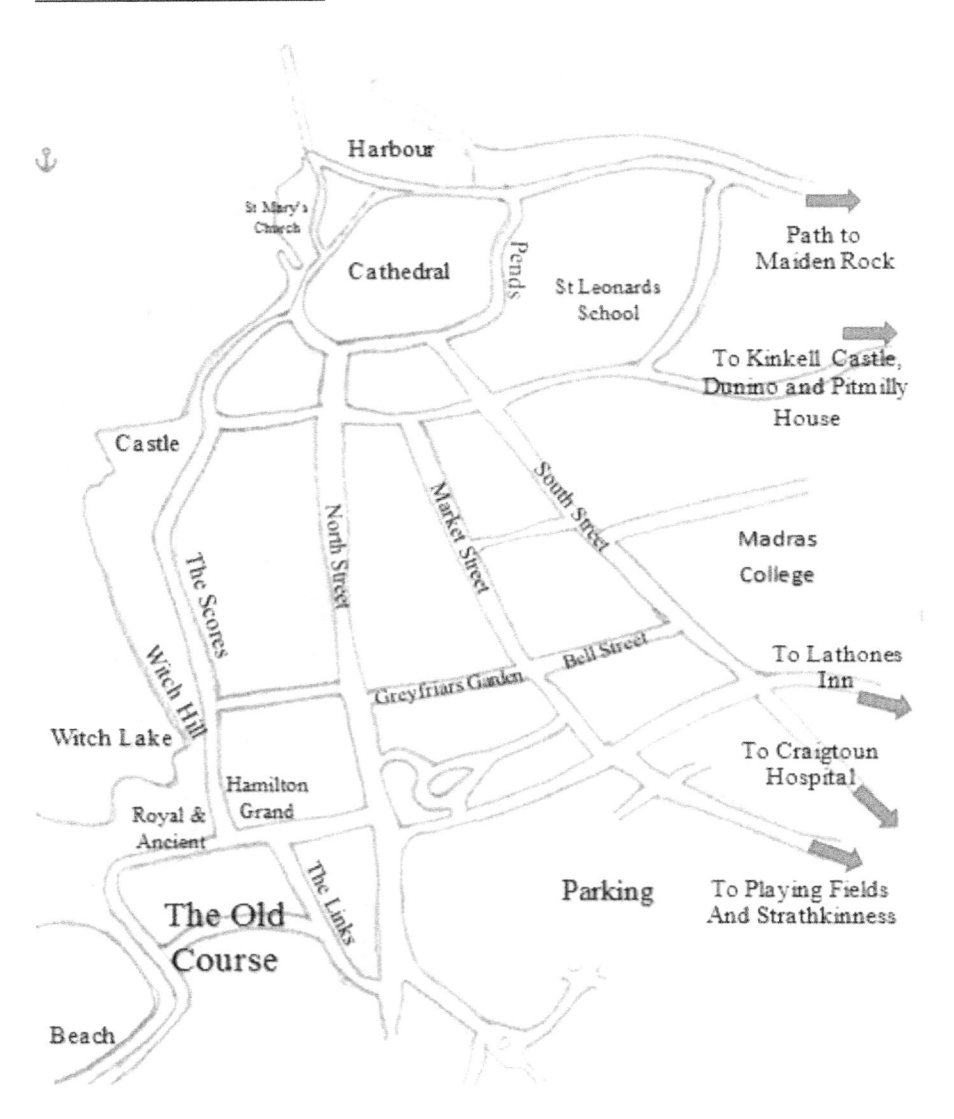

Note from the Author: The above routes are indicative only and show the direction to take from the town; please ensure full directions have been obtained prior to travelling.

With St Andrews proving to be such a draw for people from all sides of the religious spectrum, who travelled to the town in their thousands over the centuries, it is understandable that the surrounding area has also experienced its fair share of the darker side of history, which has left scars on the countryside and resulted in reputedly haunted locations. I have selected some of the more interesting stories from the immediate area, all of which can be visited relatively easily from St Andrews by car (although some of the buildings are either complete ruins or no longer exist).

PHANTOM MONKS

On the student form *'The Sinner'*, a tale from the outskirts of the town is featured. Apparently the ghostly figures of two monks were witnessed walking across the University sports fields, which are located just past the University Hall on Buchanan Gardens.

The University Sports Fields

Unusual as it would be to see monks still in the town, any suggestion of them being fellow students dressed up can be eliminated by the fact that like the phantom dog of Deans Court, the monks were walking several inches above the ground level, as though floating through the air.

They were seen to be carrying something between them, which appeared to be another monk, perhaps one of their fallen or injured brothers. The reports do not mention which direction the figures were walking, although given the history of St Andrews and the many battles, it is possible they had been either trying to get back to their monastery, or to escape from it.

THE MAIDEN ROCK

The Maiden Rock

The Maiden (or sometimes Maiden's) Rock is a natural sandstone sea stack that is around a fifteen minute walk along the coastal path towards Crail. This is a popular walk with both locals and visitors alike, with many pausing as they do so to gaze out to sea, but few know of the tragedies that have happened in these waters. When the tide is out, long strips of rocks extending out from the shore for some distance are revealed, and it is on these rocks that many ships have been lost in the past, with considerable loss of life. The Royal Commission on the Ancient and Historical Monuments of Scotland gives details of the wreck of a 19th century Brig (defined as a medium sized decked sailing vessel having two masts with square sails on both, and normally of timber construction) named the Mary that lies on the sea bed to the east of the Maiden Rock.

In October 1884, this ship was sailing from South Shields to London with a cargo of coal, when a gale drove the boat north and into St. Andrews bay. Despite anchoring, she was dragged and completely wrecked.

Local folklore tells that the rock has been long haunted by the ghost of a young lady, who visits the beach below nightly, weeping as she mourns the loss of her lover at sea. The rock is said to have been named after this spook. W.T. Linskill tells a different, and predictably far more flamboyant version of events that led to the spirit of the lady of the rock. In his book *'St. Andrews Ghost Stories'*, he claims that ancient documents were discovered in a local house and when they were examined they were found to tell a tragic story of young love. The house in which the documents were found was apparently once owned by a Frenchman, who had a daughter named Ermentrude who was gifted with great beauty. Her father had intended that Ermentrude would become a nun, however, by the age of twenty she had fallen in love with a young student named Eugene. Her father accepted the situation, and two years later the couple were preparing to be married at the cathedral when Ermentrude's cousin, Marie, came to stay. Eugene quickly fell for her, and word reached Ermentrude that they were planning to run away together. Distraught, she consulted a wise woman, who turned out to be a witch who, after hearing of her situation, gave her a potion to drink and dagger to deal with her foe.

She later took the potion that, rather than help as she had hoped, only served to increase her jealousy and anger. In a fit of rage, she entered Marie's bedchamber while she slept and drove the blade of the dagger through her heart, at which point the potions control over her was broken. Ermentrude quickly regained her senses and, realising what she had done, she fled the scene. She was never seen again, but it is believed she drowned herself at the Maiden Rock, where her ghost still walks.

KINKELL CASTLE

Kinkell Castle once stood on the cliff top around two miles from St. Andrews and was an early home to the Monypenny family (who will be discussed in more detail later in the section covering Pitmilly House). There appears to be little recorded about the history of the castle, although as the land was gifted to the Monypenny family in the twelfth century, it is likely that the building was constructed fairly soon afterwards in the mid to late 1100s. The fortified manor house overlooked the Rock and Spindle (another sea stack) and a natural harbour. Kinkell Cave is situated in the cliff face not far from where the castle stood, and archaeological investigations at the caves have revealed they had been occupied for some time by humans.

By the seventeenth century, Kinkell Castle was owned by the Hamilton family, who were sympathetic towards the Covenanters and offered them a safe home, and so it is believed that it had been Covenanters who had stayed at the cave, guided there by the Hamiltons when seeking a place of safety. In the book *History of the Parish Church of the Holy Trinity St Andrews'*, by Alexander Wynd (published 2012) it states that a number of Conventicles (open air services by banned preachers) were held in the St Andrews area and, in 1674, one was being held at Kinkell. Archbishop Sharp received word of it and, determined to crush the Covenanters and those who supported them, he ordered the Provost of St Andrews to send the Militia to the castle to capture those responsible. To his dismay, the Provost replied that he could not do as he was instructed, as the Militia were already at the castle, listening to the preacher! This is perhaps another demonstration of how much the people of the town disliked Sharp.

Some years later, Hamilton was eventually taken captive for his support of the Covenanters, and though he escaped with his life, he was stripped of his land. By 1775, the maps of the area showed the castle as being ruins and today nothing remains of it. The Castle Golf course was built on the site of Kinkell Castle (hence the name of the course) and there was some expectation that the remains of the castle would be found during the formation of the course, but unfortunately this was not to be the case. Prior to their loss, the ruins were said to have been haunted by the ghost of a woman who walked through the castle. This phantom was believed to be the spirit of Lady Hamilton, returning to her home where she and her husband defied the authorities and stood up for what they believed in. There have been no reports of sighting on the golf course that I am aware of, but it is a relatively new course, and so time will tell whether she is still there and if the golfers encounter the phantom figure.

The Coastline at Kinkell where the castle once stood

DUNINO DEN AND THE PHANTOM VILLAGE

Readers may recall that I earlier told the story of a young woman named Alison Pearson, a local 'wise woman', who was believed to have gained her knowledge of the herbal healing remedies from the faeries, resulting in her help being much sought after, but which would eventually see her accused of witchcraft and burned at the stake. The location where she is said to have had her first encounter with the faerie folk is a site at the village of Dunino, around four miles from St. Andrews.

It was here, in a wooded area on the hillside leading down to the river that Alison encountered the spirit of her cousin, in the form of a green man, although it was a religious site long before Alison's time and remains a fascinating and mystical place to this day. There is evidence it was a place of worship for the Druids, a religious faction within the Celts who first arrived in Britain about 1500 B.C. Unfortunately, like the ancient Picts before them, the Druids did not keep accurate written records and so what is known about them is pieced together from other sources and archaeological evidence. It is known that when Christianity was first brought to Britain, the leaders sought to stamp out all existing religions, and so it is possible that what has been written about the Druids may have been influenced in a negative way by the early Christians, keen to dispel the idea of Druid gods and convert everyone to Christianity. In Dunino, the church was built on the hilltop looking down on the Druid's Den, no doubt to try to show its superiority as the 'higher' religion, looking down on others.

The den can be accessed by following a path from the church carpark down the side of the cemetery and into the wooded area. A rocky outcrop overlooking the river reveals the location of the den. This section of rock has a cylindrical hole cut into it and the shape of a foot carved beside it. This is believed to have been a sacrificial pool, into which the blood of the sacrifices would be drained before the body was thrown down into the river below. There is nothing to suggest there was ever any human sacrifices made, and certainly, the river is not large enough to have been able to carry away the body of anything much more than a small animal.

The Sacrificial Pool and Steps to the Den

To the side of this outcrop, a narrow, steep staircase is carved into the rock which takes you down to the den. Great care must be taken on the steps, remember they are potentially thousands of years old and have been considerably worn. As you reach the bottom though, take time to look at the rock face, where there are several ancient symbols carved into the stone. Most of the trees within the den have ribbons tied to the branches, and there are painted seashells, wicker symbols and other messages left throughout by visitors for their own personal reasons. The rock face is covered in coins, dating back many years and from numerous different countries, all inserted into the cracks in the cliff, presumably as an offer to the gods or spirits, depending on the individuals belief. Despite being badly worn over the centuries, a ten foot high Celtic cross that is carved into the stone still dominates the site. A second rocky outcrop is more noticeable from down within the den. This is known as 'the pulpit', and it is believed it is from here, overlooking those in the den and across to the sacrificial pool, that the high priests would have delivered their sermons. A cavern exists below this rock, and this may have been where the wise woman would have practiced her medicine.

There is another unusual story connected with this site that does not just tell of an encounter with a ghost, but of a whole phantom town! Folklore has it that many centuries ago a traveller was trying to find the church to seek shelter on a stormy night, when he lost his way. He came across a small village of little more than a few houses, but enough to offer him a dry place to wait until the storm passed. While looking around to seek someone who could assist him, he spotted an elderly couple at the door of one of the houses. While the thought crossed the traveller's mind to ask them if he could come into their cottage to shelter from the rain and dry himself, something stopped him. Perhaps it was the way the couple simply stood in the rain and stared at him in silence, or perhaps it was a sixth sense warning him against approaching them. Whatever the reason was, the traveller turned back instead and this time found the correct path that led to the church.

After changing into dry clothes and warming himself in the church, he began chatting to the minister and referred to the unusual manner of the couple at the nearby village. His comments were met with a confused expression. He was told there is, and never has been, such a village in the location that he described. It seems the traveller was very fortunate in his decision not to approach or to enter any of these ghostly houses.

PITMILLY HOUSE

Five miles outside St Andrews, just before the quaint fishing village of Kingsbarns, a high stone wall hides the partial ruins of a once impressive manor house. The property has a long history involving some of the most influential people of the area, but in 1936, the history was to take a dark twist, when the first of many unexplained activities took place that would ultimately lead to the building being destroyed.

The mansion house originally stood in expansive grounds (which the road now runs through) and was the home to the Monypenny family, who took possession of the lands in 1211. In the book *'Discovering Fife'* by Raymond Lamont-Brown, published in 1988, a curious local legend is told as to the origin of the Monypenny family name, which is said to date back to the time of King MacBeth (the real king, not the character made famous in Shakespeare's play). In the year 1040, King Duncan 1st attempted to impose his authority over the independent dynasty of Moray, a region in the north of Scotland. In his quest, he was twice defeated by the armies of the ruler of Moray, the Earl of Orkney.

On 14th August 1040, King Duncan was killed on the battlefield by his own cousin, Macbeth, who had sided with the Earl of Orkney. Seizing the opportunity through the family connection, MacBeth subsequently claimed King Duncan's throne for himself. Duncan's wife and children, including his young son and rightful heir, Malcolm, fled to England for their own safety and on the journey, Malcolm asked a stranger for a loan of a few pennies. The stranger replied 'Nae Sire, no a few pennies, but mony (many) pennies' and provided them with enough money to make their escape. Several years later, Malcolm, who had grown into a strong young man, returned to Scotland with an army and defeated Macbeth, before taking his rightful place as King Malcolm III. He never forgot the kindness of the stranger who aided their escape, and he set about tracking him down. He gifted the kindly man land and property in gratitude for his assistance, and gave him the family name of 'Monypenny', after the reply he had given many years prior, and the name was used from that point onwards.

The property, which dated back to the middle ages with a later Georgian wing added towards the end of the eighteenth century, was the home of the Monypenny family for over seven centuries until, in 1930, Captain J.A. Jefferey purchased Pitmilly House. Jefferey had in fact been born at the house, which no doubt influenced his decision to purchase it. He soon moved into Pitmilly, along with his wife, Alison, and two children, Thomas Ivan (born 1915) and Mary Elizabeth (born 1924). Two maids who had been in their service for many years, also joined them to oversee the day to day running of the property. Initially, everything seemed fine and the family soon settled into the luxurious country living that the house offered until, in 1936, everything changed. While the family were sitting at the table having dinner, a flaming piece of coal suddenly appeared in the middle of the table from nowhere. It seems that the burning coal did not cause any damage to the property on this occasion, but it certainly unnerved the family who questioned where it had come from.

This was the start of one of the longest known cases of poltergeist activity in history. This, along with the destructive power of the unseen force, attracted the interest of renowned psychic, paranormal researcher and author, Harry Price (who famously investigated the incidents at the Borley Rectory). Price was so taken by the happenings at the house, that he devoted an entire chapter to Pitmilly in his 1945 book *'Poltergeist Over England'* (which sees odd, given that Pitmilly is in Scotland!).

The Society for Phsychical Research (SPR) have produced information on the numerous incidents that occurred at the house, which included ornaments being broken or moved, paintings falling off the walls, heavy items of furniture moving by themselves (often in full view of witnesses) and the family being unable to leave any water in the bedrooms as, as soon as they left the room, the water would be emptied over the bed. The SPR provides details of an interview given by Thomas Ivan to Radio 4 in 1967, in which he described life at the house. He stated the incidents started when he was 'comparatively young'. As he would have been twenty-one years old in 1936, when the incident with the coal appearing at the table is documented to have occurred, this would seem to suggest that that was not in fact the first incident, or that it occurred earlier than documented. He also gave details of witnessing a heavy bronze ornament float along the hallway and hit him in his stomach, wardrobes lifting up into the air before crashing back down to the floor, and more burning lumps of coal appearing at random, setting fire to the curtains.

Other incidents witnessed by several people are said to have been paintings that lined the wall of the staircase lifting and rotating on their hanging chains, a heavy wardrobe tilting to forty five degrees and hovering, as though defying gravity, and a heavy vase floating down the hallway, before turning at right angles out into the garden, where it came to rest.

In 1940, the building suffered considerable fire damage. Curiously, when the fire brigade arrived, they found that there were several fires, and their report indicates that in eight or nine rooms fires had all started just below ceiling level, all at the same time. One can only speculate whether this was another consequence of burning pieces of coal appearing around the house, or something else altogether. It is difficult to come up with a probable cause for so many fires starting, simultaneously, in the same location but in different rooms. It is however known that the case was thoroughly investigated and no human cause could be identified as on 8th April 1942, *The Press and Journal* Newspaper published a story titled 'Damage by Ghost - £400'. The article tells that, for probably the first time in history, an insurance company had paid out on a claim for damage caused by a ghost. The insurers had investigated the fire extensively and are said to have been certain that the fires were not started by the occupants of the house, but also certain that they had not been caused by an accident. With no other evidence, they had no option but to pay. The family were represented in the presentation of the claim by their solicitor, who, according to the SPR, had been witness himself to some of the unusual incidents at the house, including vases lifting into the air where they floated before falling.

Séances and exorcisms were also reported to have been held at the house in an attempt to make contact with whatever was responsible for the unexplained incidents, but these were inconclusive. One bishop who attended to carry out an exorcism is said to have been sitting beside a fireplace as he prepared. He had placed his hat on his lap and could only watch in horror as it was raised into the air and thrown into the burning fire by an unseen entity.

Other newspapers ran similar stories regarding the insurance claim and most detailed some of the earlier incidents and so, for the first time, the strange phenomena was starting to become public knowledge. The house had by this time been requisitioned and used to station Polish troops through the war years. Things appeared to have calmed down, although in fact it would seem incidents continued but they were just not being talked about as much. Captain Jefferey had died in 1941, and his ghost is said to have been seen walking through the house, and there were still claims that items of furniture were being moved. The SPR suggests that an article titled 'No Rest at the Mansion' published in *the American Weekly* in July 1942, relates to the happenings experienced by the troops at Pitmilly, although the house is not directly named.

After the war ended, the house was returned to Thomas and Mary (their mother had also passed by this time) and they subsequently sold it. In 1947, there were several articles in the press, such as that published in *the Sunday Post* on 22nd June, titled 'House With "Ghost" Now A Hotel'. These articles re-told some of the earlier poltergeist activities at the house, and also introduced the tale of the Green Lady, who they said haunted the building. The Green Lady seems to be a far older haunting and was a peaceful figure, not connected with the destructive activities of the Poltergeist. The only reference I have found that may relate to this ghost is an incident mentioned by the SPR when a pair of long gloves were left to dry in front of the fire. When the owner returned to collect them, she was horrified to find that they were being worn and held in front of the fire as though the wearer was warming their hands, but there was no person visible. There was no apparent malice in this incident and so perhaps this was the Green Lady taking a liking to the gloves (maybe they were green).

The hotel operated relatively successfully for some years, with fewer reported incidents, other than bottles of alcohol being found completely drained but with their seals intact. With tales of the strange occurrences continuing to spread and competition in the area growing, the hotel eventually closed in 1967 and the land was sold to the local farmer. Sadly, the house was completely demolished and the site cleared and turned over to cultivation. Some of the stone is believed to have been used to build houses in the village of Kingsbarns, and it would be interesting to establish which houses used the stone and whether there has been any reported incidents within them. No trace of Pitmilly House remains today, other than the ruins of the stables and lodge.

The Stable Block at Pitmilly House

What caused the poltergeist activity at Pitmilly has been the subject of several investigations but remains a mystery. These incidents are often related to teenage children, particularly if there is anguish in their lives, and there are claims that Alison Jefferey would not allow her daughter to attend school, insisting instead she was taught in the house. With her brother being sent out to the local school and then joining the army, Mary's confinement to the house no doubt led to frustration and anger which could have been the spark needed to start the Poltergeist activity, but with incidents being reported over a thirty year period, they cannot all be attributed to Mary.

Another cause for incidents such as these is the spirits of those who have died suddenly and unexpectedly, resulting in them not realising they are dead and reacting angrily or causing some form of negative energy in the atmosphere. A search of the newspaper archives reveals there were two such incidents with connections to the house, both occurring around the time the activity started. The first was reported in the *Dundee Courier* on

17th December 1931 and tells of a motor cycle accident on a road close to the house, in which a local blacksmith, William Grubb Bissett, lost control on a corner and was thrown from his bike. Bissett was found by John MacDougall, who was also on a motor cycle and had to swerve to avoid the body on the road, resulting in him crashing his own bike and sustaining minor injuries. MacDougall, who was employed as a chauffeur at nearby Pitmilly House, raised the alarm (no doubt at Pitmilly), but when medical assistance arrived it was found that Bissett had sustained a fractured skull and would have died instantly. Although this incident occurred five years prior to the normally quoted date for the start of activity at Pitmilly, the reader will recall from the comments made by Thomas in his 1967 interview, that the incidents may have in fact started earlier.

The second occurrence also relates to a motor cycle accident. The story was again carried by the *Dundee Courier*, published on 18th July 1934, and tells of the death of a man named Thomas Middleton, who died instantly when he lost control of his bike on the corner outside the house grounds and struck a telegraph pole. His brother, James Middleton, had also been on the bike but had thrown himself clear before the impact and survived. James Middleton was employed as the gardener at Pitmilly, and his brother had been visiting him from England for a short holiday.

There is also another potential cause for the disturbances. There were no known incidents prior to Captain Jefferey purchasing the house, and it is curious to note that there reports that his ghost was witnessed at the house shortly after his death. Perhaps the Captain had done something at the house that brought the poltergeist to his home, and his ghost returned to either deal with whatever he had awoken, or to conceal his secret?

Whatever the cause for the occurrences at Pitmilly House, it is to this day one of the most extensive and fascinating poltergeist cases, and while some have attempted to explain it through physical causes, all seem to conclude that much of what happened, along with the reason why, remains unexplained.

THE INN AT LATHONES

The Inn at Lathones

A ten minute drive from the centre of St. Andrews towards the small town of Largoward will take you to the Lathones Inn. Surrounded by open countryside, this four hundred year old eatery offers quality dining and luxury accommodation, which is quite different from its past. The oldest part of the inn is the former stable block, which was constructed around 1603 and has now been converted and renovated to accommodate the bar area and to provide more informal dining. The building at the front, closest to the road, was constructed in the late 1600s. One of the most interesting features in the inn is a marriage stone, built into the fabric of the building above a fireplace, which commemorates the wedding of Iona Kirk and Ewan Lindsay in 1718. The couple ran the inn for eighteen years, until Iona tragically died in 1736. Local folklore states that the wedding stone cracked on the day she died, and that Ewan died a short while later of unknown causes, said to have been a broken heart.

The inn was also said to have been a favourite stopping point for a local highwayman known as 'Wee Mad MacGregor' (due to his short stature) during the eighteenth century. He would plunder the surrounding area and, whenever his ill-gotten gains allowed, he would stop at the inn to drink and eat. By this time the inn mainly provided facilities for the drovers (men who took the horses and cattle to market), and so the highwayman would not have appeared out of place there.

By the mid nineteenth century, the inn was used by the miners from the coal pits that had been established beneath the surrounding fields, and it even provided these hard working men with their own golf course. With the pits flooding in the 1920s, they were eventually closed after one hundred years, bringing the local mining industry to an end. Since then the inn has undergone extensive, sympathetic renovation to restore much of the original features and charm and it still offers a warm welcome to weary travellers.

The figure of a grey lady, along with her horse, have been seen in the bar area (the former stables). The belief is that the lady is the ghost of Iona Kirk, still stabling her horse as she returns to the inn that she so happily ran with her husband. Other reported unexplained incidents are the fire tools hanging on the companion set starting to swing with no visible force being applied and, on occasions, the companion set seems to move, unseen, from one side of the fireplace to the other. Doors and windows are also said to open and close, again with no visible force, and the sound of a crying baby has been heard from one of the upstairs rooms.

CRAIGTOUN HOSPITAL

Perched on a hillside, with stunning views down over St Andrews and out to the sea beyond, the former Craigtoun Maternity Hospital occupies what must be one of the best sites around the town, and the building itself is sufficiently magnificent to do the location justice.

The hospital is a converted mansion house, which was built in the early twentieth century, although this is not the first of the grand buildings that have occupied this site. The earliest manor, known as Mount Melville House, was constructed there in 1698 for General George Melville of Strathkinness. This original house had been extensively remodelled/rebuilt by the late 18th century for General Robert Melville, a distinguished military man and a keen botanist, who was responsible for establishing the formal gardens throughout the estate. The gardens were added to and enhanced by later owners resulting in Historic Scotland categorising them as being 'outstanding' for their historical importance.

By 1821, the original mansion house had been completely replaced for John Whyte-Melville, and the gardens were re-laid forming a north and south park, with Mount Melville House being on a ridge in the centre. The property remained in the ownership of the Melville family until 1901, when it was sold to Dr James Younger, from the Younger brewing family. Dr Younger carried out extensive remodelling of the estate, including having a new house built, which was designed on the original but constructed in distinctive pink sandstone leading Historic Scotland to describe it as being a 'huge pink sandstone Jacobean chateau'. In 1920, considerable landscaping work was carried out which included the creation of lakes, complete with a model village on its own island. In 1947, the house and its land were sold to Fife Council, who renamed it, Craigtoun. A country park was established on part of the grounds to allow the public to visit and enjoy the estate. The mansion house was converted into a maternity hospital and the remainder of the estate was turned over to farmland. Constantly rising maintenance and running costs made the hospital increasingly difficult to manage and, after a brief spell as a home for the elderly while a new hospital facility was being built in the town, the maternity hospital closed. Although Craigtoun Country Park remained in the ownership of the Council and continued to operate, the house and three hundred and thirty acres of parkland were sold to the Kohler Company, owners of the Old Course Hotel and Hamilton Grand. A new golf course, known as the Duke's Course, was built on the parkland and there were plans for the house to be converted into a golf club offering exclusive accommodation. Unfortunately, the changes in the economic climate have so far resulted in the building remaining empty and boarded with no sign of any work being undertaken. On the Duke's course website, there remains mention of their intention to restore the building to its former glory, to comprise of a leisure and health club, along with exclusive apartments and suites. Based on the restoration carried out by the Kohler Co. at the Hamilton Grand, Mount Melville House is likely to become a very impressive building once again.

Mount Melville House

Tales of the house being haunted by a nurse or midwife have persisted throughout the buildings use as a maternity hospital, although details are scarce and mainly passed down through word of mouth, with her ghostly figure being seen walking the long corridors and gliding from room to room. The reason for a nurse haunting the building are unclear (unless she really loved her job and wanted to return!). The spirit is said to have been seen on many occasions both by visitors and staff and, despite thelack of documentation, tales of her presence have continued through generations.

Another, more sinister tale relates to a statue within the grounds of the house depicting a beautiful woman holding a smiling baby. Closer inspection of the statue however reveals the baby has cloven feet.

Statue of the maiden and baby

Some will tell you that the statue is Pan, the Greek God, as a child in his mother's arms. Curiously, despite there being numerous statues within the grounds, this particular one was placed in a more secluded location, and there is local folklore to explain this. It is said that long ago, a maid fell pregnant to one of the senior men of the house. Her lover agreed for her to go through with the pregnancy, but it was to be kept secret, as it would have caused embarrassment to the family, especially since the father was married. The story surrounding the birth of the child varies.

The gentler version tells that the father was so taken with the child, that he had a statue of the mother and baby carved which he placed in an out of the way position in the gardens. His wife however found the statue and the story of his affair came out, resulting in him having the statue altered to have hooves for feet, to symbolise that the birth was as a result of his misdemeanour. The maid, unable to cope with the shame, committed suicide by throwing herself from the roof of the building. The more macabre version tells that the baby was born with club foot, a deformity that makes the foot point down and inwards, with the soles facing backwards. Convinced that this was a sign that the baby was evil or demonic due to it being born out of wedlock and as a result of his sin, the father had the baby murdered. When the child's mother discovered what he had done, she was so distraught she killed herself. Full of remorse for his actions, the father had the stature carved in their memory.

Common to both versions of the story is that the ghost of the maid still walks through the house and gardens, seeking her lost child. The sound of a woman crying has also been heard in the house, which people believe to be the maid.

The Dukes Golf Course, formerly part of the estate, also claims to have a ghost. This is the phantom coach of Archbishop Sharp that is seen crossing the course, along with the sound of a woman screaming in the distance, believed to be the Archbishop's daughter. The story of Archbishop Sharp will be covered in the next section.

GREGOR STEWART

MAGUS MUIR AND ARCHBISHOP SHARP

This final tale is one of deception, double-crossing and murder, which has several ghosts associated with it. Around three miles outside St. Andrews, a small area of natural woodland named Magus Muir sits in the hillside across from the village of Strathkinness and offers a quiet and peaceful walk. Towards the end of the path an unusual stone pyramid shaped monument comes into view. Difficult as it may be to imagine in the tranquil setting, this marks the spot where Archbishop James Sharp was violently murdered in front of his daughter.

Archbishop Sharp's Monument

Scotland had been going through religious turmoil for decades, and it was the actions taken by Archbishop Sharp that led him to be deeply unpopular and ultimately resulted in his death. The Kingdoms of Scotland, England and Ireland had been united when King James VI of Scotland inherited the English and Irish thrones in 1603, and he became the first monarch to style himself as the King of Great Britain and Ireland. Despite the Union of the Crowns, the King faced considerable obstacles in England and there were several plots made against him, the best known being the gunpowder plot in which Guy Fawkes was involved. Many of the difficulties had their foundation in religion, with King James believing that the king should have complete control over everything, including religion. This did not meet with the agreement of either the Catholic faith, which believes the Pope is the head of the church, or Presbyterianism, in which Jesus Christ is the head, and so he faced much resistance to his plans.

After the death of King James, the throne was passed to his son, Charles 1st, who continued with his father's religious beliefs leading to a lengthy dispute with the English Parliament. Unable to resolve the issues and frustrated at the lack of co-operation, King Charles dissolved the English Parliament in 1629 and continued to rule without it for eleven years. During this time, he tried to enforce worshiping at the Church of England, which led to the signing of the National Covenant in Scotland in 1638. This revived an earlier document, known as 'the King's Confession', signed in 1581, in which the King and the people promised to maintain the Presbyterian Church. The new National Covenant swore allegiance to the King, but added that there could be no interference from the King or the Catholic system in the direct relationship between the people of Scotland and God.

War followed, with King James forming an army to forcibly retake control of the Scottish church. In Scotland, those who had signed the National Covenant (known as the Covenanters) gathered an army to fight the king's forces and they met in February 1639, marking the start of what became known as the First Bishops' War. In reality, with the king being unpopular and there being little desire among the English to go to war with Scotland again, he had been unable to gather a particularly large or formidable force. When faced with the Covenanters fully equipped and motivated army, they stood little chance and by March, the Covenanters had retaken Edinburgh Castle with little blood loss. By June the King's forces had withdrawn and the Treaty of Berwick was signed that brought an, albeit temporary, truce between the two sides.

By 1640, the King was once again preparing for war, this time, he hoped, with the backing of the reformed English Parliament. It seems his earlier action against the Parliament had not however been forgotten, and they refused to provide the funds to form an army or to go into battle, and so the King struggled to take any action. Rather than wait, the Covenanters took the fight to the King and marched on England, marking the start of the Second Bishops' War. After they successfully took control of the city of Newcastle the King was forced to again accept a humiliating defeat.

The people of England were becoming increasingly dissatisfied with the King, and civil war broke out, with the English Parliament seeking help from Scotland to fight the royal forces. The Scottish authorities sought to secure religious settlement in return for their military assistance and, in 1643, a document known as the Solemn League and Covenant was signed, following which a Scottish army was sent to fight alongside the English. In the meantime, Scottish Ministers were sent to meet with the English Parliament to offer advice on the reformation of the English and Irish churches. In 1646 King James surrendered to the Scottish Army, and he was handed over to the English Parliament the following year, before being executed for treason in 1649. By this time, Oliver Cromwell and his New Model Army were the decisive force in England, and he successfully declared the country as a republic, known as the Commonwealth of England.

A month after the execution of King Charles, the Scottish Parliament proclaimed his son, Charles II, to be King. As England by this time had become a Republic, the English Parliament did not recognise the King, and instead Cromwell led England. Angered by the action of the Scots in recognising Charles as the new king, he brought his army north to do battle with the Scottish Royalists, with the final battle taking place at Worcester in 1651. King Charles II fled to mainland Europe and Cromwell effectively became the ruler of England, Scotland, Ireland and Wales, with him being sworn in as Lord Protector in 1653, a role that he held until his death in 1658. Following his death, his son, Richard, took over the role of Lord Protector.

During this time, Archbishop Sharp had been a minister in the Scottish Presbyterian Church, and offered his support to the Covenanters. Unknown to them, Sharp was aware that the death of Oliver Cromwell was likely to signal change, and he had secret plans to safeguard his own position, regardless of how devastating the result of his actions would be on others. Richard Cromwell lacked his father's authoritarian leadership style and his control of the country quickly slipped, allowing King Charles II to return and he was restored as the monarch in 1660. Following the King's return from Europe, Sharp maintained his support for the Presbyterian Church. Knowing that Sharp had been in contact with the King, his ongoing support led his peers to believe that the King was going to honour the Presbyterian religious settlement in Scotland. They soon discovered this was not the case, and King Charles II once again moved to enforce the Episcopacy in Scotland, which would see him made leader of the church. Sharp at that point revealed that he had changed his allegiance and supported the King, who in turn granted him the position of Archbishop of St Andrews in 1661.

The Covenanters continued to oppose any change to the church and as a result, they were forced from their church buildings to be replaced with ministers who supported the new system. Determined that their voices would be heard, the expelled ministers started to preach in fields and forests all over the country. In an attempt to stop people attending these makeshift sermons, a law was passed that ordered the people to attend church on a Sunday or face fines, and threatened punishment against the ejected ministers if they continued to preach in the open air, along with anyone in attendance. A brutal campaign followed against the covenanters, with Archbishop Sharp being one of the main persecutors of his former fellow allies, who faced horrific treatment, torture and death. He was also responsible for reintroducing the Court of High Commission, in which those accused could be sentenced to death with no right of appeal, an action that would ensure the Covenanters could be dealt with swiftly and decisively.

On 3rd May 1679, Archbishop Sharp was returning from Edinburgh to his home at the New Inns in St Andrews, accompanied by his daughter. Unknown to him, a small group of Covenanters had gathered at the nearby village of Ceres where they were planning an attack on the Sherriff of Cupar. They were however tipped off that the Archbishop's coach had been seen, and with him representing a far more significant target, they set on their way to intercept the coach. At Magus Muir, they caught up with the coach before surrounding it and forcing it to stop. Upon realising that the Archbishop's daughter was with him, they ordered Sharp out of the carriage, as they did not mean his daughter any harm. Sharp however refused and stayed inside until eventually the covenanters forced their way in, shooting and stabbing him before dragging him out and throwing him to the ground, where they continued their attack until he was dead.

Engraved by H. Bourne from the original painting by Sir William Allan, R. A., London. c. 1840

With the authorities keen to be seen to act swiftly, but with the murderers in hiding, in an ironic system of false justice, five covenanters who were captured at the Battle of Bothwell Bridge in June 1679 were charged with the killing. The fact they had been nowhere near Magus Muir and had played no part in the assassination was deemed irrelevant, they were guilty merely on the basis that they were Covenanters, and so must be concealing those who committed the crime. The men were hung at Magus Muir on 25th November 1679, and they were buried at the site in unconsecrated ground.

The phantom coach of Archbishop Sharp is reported to continue the journey from Magus Muir to St. Andrews, with reports of it being seen from the Strathkinness Low Road, travelling across the fields, following the route of the original roadway. In her book *'A Haunting of Ghosts'*, Helen Cook tells of a sighting that she had heard about that took place just before World War II. A St Andrews man was said to have been driving home, accompanied by a friend, along the Low Road. It was around 3 a.m. but a bright summer morning and so there was enough light to allow them to make out another vehicle travelling in front of them. The man commented at how foolish the driver of the other vehicle must be as they were driving with no lights on. As they caught up and considered whether it was safe to pass on the narrow road, they were amazed to see the vehicle turn and continue across the fields where the old coaching road used to be, until it finally disappeared into the darkness. If this was an encounter with Archbishop Sharp's coach, then those inside the car should consider themselves fortunate, as a sighting of the coach is normally believed to be an omen, warning of imminent bad luck.

As discussed earlier in the book, the coach is also heard and seen both in South Street and in the Pends as it continues its ghostly trip back to Sharp's residence. Curiously it seems that the only area where witnessing the coach is deemed bad luck is on the Strathkinness Low Road, and it is possible this belief is due to some general confusion with another phantom coach also seen near the town, as told by W.T. Linskill in a tale called *'The True Story of the Phantom Coach'*.

In this encounter, which would have taken place when coaches were a common means of transport, Linskill states that two tramps had been making their way back into St Andrews on a stormy night, when an unusual looking coach passed them and stopped. The door swung open and a white hand emerged before beckoning the men to come forwards, as though inviting them into the coach. One of the tramps instinctively did so, rushing to get out of the rain and grateful for the lift. Before the other man could decide whether to follow his companion, the door of the coach closed and it continued on its way, leaving him standing on the roadside. He was never to see his friend alive again, with his body being found in St. Andrews bay some months later.

There is a suggestion that this coach may in fact be that of David Haxton, one of the covenanters involved in the murder of Archbishop Sharp and who was eventually captured a year after the killing. Haxton suffered a horrific death at the Mercat Cross in Edinburgh, which is documented in the 1829 book *'The History of the Sufferings of the Church of Scotland from the Restoration to the Revolution'*, by Rev. Robert Wodrow, which describes the means of execution as follows:

'That his body be drawn backward on a hurdle to the Mercat Cross; that there be a high scaffold erected a little above the Cross, where, in the first place, his right hand is to be struck off and, after some time, his left hand; then he is to be hanged up, and cut down alive, his bowels to be taken out, and his heart shown to the people by the hangman; then his heart and his bowels to be burned in a fire prepared for that purpose on the scaffold; that, afterwards, his head be cut off, and his body divided into four quarters; his head to be fixed on the Netherbow; one of his quarters with both his hands to be affixed at St. Andrews, another quarter at Glasgow, a third at Leith, a fourth at Burntisland; that none presume to be in mourning for him, or any coffin brought; that no person be suffered to be on the scaffold with him, save the two bailies, the executioner and his servants; that he be allowed to pray to God Almighty, but not to speak to the people.'

The book goes on to tell that when Haxton reached the Mercat Cross, he was already dying from his wounds, no doubt caused as a result of the battles he had been involved in prior to his capture, and the torture sessions that he would have endured at the hands of the authorities. The description of his death is as follows:

'After his hands were cut off, which he endured with great firmness and patience, he was drawn up to the top of the gallows with a pulley, and, when choked a little, let down alive within the hangman's reach, who opened his breast with a knife and pulled out his heart, which moved upon the scaffold. Then the executioner stuck his knife in it, carried it about the stage, and showed it to the spectators, crying 'Here is the heart of a traitor'. And then the rest of the sentence was executed.'

From the above, it seems Haxton's still beating heart was allowed to hang from the gaping wound in his chest for a period of time, during which he still hung, choking, from the scaffold. With the brutality of his death, it is understandable why some would suggest that Haxton's soul would not be at rest. My own view however is that it would be unlikely for him to be in a coach responsible for taking those who enter to their death, unless there was of course something in the victims past that was not documented that might make them targets. No doubt, the identity of the passenger in the coach that beckons travellers to enter will however remain a mystery. There is also a tale covering final stages of its journey that says the coach is seen in the vicinity of the West Sands road, pulled by four horses and heading towards the sea, before disappearing with a 'puff' of blue smoke leaving only the smell of sulphur, a smell often associated with ghosts.

ADDITIONAL INFORMATION AND OTHER PUBLICATIONS

I do hope you have enjoyed this collection of tales from the town of St Andrews, which from first starting to collect the stories, to carrying out the research and finally compiling the information into one volume, is the result of over twenty years of work. As a Paranormal Researcher, I am always interested to hear reader's stories and personal experiences. I am currently collecting ghost stories from Edinburgh, Glasgow and the Highlands as well as starting to look into the fascinating locations in the United States of America and Australia. Other titles I am working on include tales of the Devil in Britain, Vampires of the UK and Scottish Folklore. I post regular updates on my blog at www.gstewartauthor.com and on Twitter @gstewart_author so please follow me and use these pages to contact me.

While maps have been provided in the book, I am more than happy to arrange private tours for small to medium groups of visitors to the town. If you are interested, please contact me through my blog.

Also by G Stewart

Compiled by paranormal investigator Gregor Stewart, this new book contains a chilling range of spooky tales from around Kirkcaldy. From haunted public houses, which have left both customers and staff terrified, to the ruins of the ancient Ravenscraig Castle, which still attract a mysterious visitor many years after their death, this collection of ghostly goings-on, phantom footsteps and playful poltergeists is sure to appeal to everyone interested in the paranormal and the history of Fife's largest town. Richly illustrated with over fifty images, Haunted Kirkcaldy is guaranteed to make your blood run cold.

Scotland is well known for being one of the most haunted countries in the world, but alongside the famous locations are many less well-known places, with equally eerie and horrific stories.

Although some of the better-known stories are touched on, this book focuses on the less well-known locations and rather than just re-tell the stories, the author has personally visited each site. Some are locations known to be haunted, in which case the book provides some history and details of the reported hauntings, along with the author's own experience and any unexplained photographs.

In the year 1563, Mary, Queen of Scots, passed Scotland's Witchcraft Act. The act not only made witchcraft illegal, but to consult with or defend a witch was also illegal. And so the witch hunts began. By the time the act was repealed in 1736, around 4000 ordinary people had been accused, tortured, convicted and executed. They were all innocent. Or were they?

When Peggy Stuart learns she shares her name with a notorious witch from the witch trials of the late 1600s in Scotland, she feels a desire to find out more information. Little did she know that her actions would lead to the Resurrection of the witch, who has lain dormant for over 300 years, waiting for the day she was released to once again unleash her powers on an unsuspecting world.

Finding that modern weapons are useless and, unable to control the witch, drastic action is considered by the government to try to stop her. Peggy and her partner, Matt Taylor, a historian at the local university and an expert in mythology must work together to try to discover her secret and how to stop her before the authorities carry out their devastating plan.

BIBLIOGRAPHY

Books and Publications

Anon, *Queen Mary's House*, W. C. Henderson & Son Ltd, 1977

Anon, *Strange Tales of Bygone Fife*, Lang Syne Publishers, 1976

Bonthrone, Eila, *Fife and its Folk; A Key to the "Kingdom"*, C J Cousland & Sons, Edinburgh, 1951

Chalmers, Robert, *Domestic Annals of Scotland: From the Reformation to the Revolution*, W & R Chalmers, Edinburgh, 1874

Cook, Helen, *A Haunting of Ghosts and an Unsolved Mystery of St Andrews*, David Winter and Son Ltd, 1983

Duncan, Ishbel MacDonald, *St Andrews, a short walking tour*, Available Online at http://ishbel.host.cs.st-andrews.ac.uk/StATour.pdf, Accessed 29th November 2014

Dunbar, John. G., *Scottish Royal Palaces*, Tuckwell Press Ltd, 1999

Evans, M.S, *Castles and Churches in Fife*, The Dolphin Press, Glenrothes, 1998

Fleming, David Hay, *Handbook to St Andrews and Neighbourhood*, J & G Inness, 1897

Geddie, John, *The Fringes of Fife*, W&R Chalmers, Edinburgh and London, New and Enlarged Edition, 1927

Gordon, Margaret Maria, *The Home Life of Sir David Brewster*, David Douglas, Edinburgh, 1881

Grierson, James, *Delineations of St. Andrews*, G. S. Tullis, Cupar, 1833

Grierson, James, *Saint Andrews As It Was And As It Is*, G. S. Tullis, Cupar, 1838

Lamont-Brown, Raymond, *Discovering Fife*, John Donald Publishing Ltd, Edinburgh, 1988

Linskill, W.T., *St Andrews Ghost Stories*, J & G Inness, St Andrews 1911

Kingshill, Sophia, *The Lore of Scotland: A guide to Scottish Legends*, Random House, 2009

Kolek, Ron and Wood, Maureen, *A Ghost a Day: 365 true tales of the Spectral, Supernatural, and Just Plain Scary*, Adams Media, 2010

Lyon, C.J., *The History of St Andrews: Ancient and Modern*, The Edinburgh Printing and Publishing Co, 1838

Lang, Andrew, *The History of Scotland – Volume 5*, Jazzybee Verlang, 2012

Lang, Theo, *The King's Scotland; The Kingdom of Fife*, Hodder and Stoughton, London, 1951

Leighton, John. M, *History of the County of Fife*, Joseph Swan, Glasgow, 1811

Oliphant, Margaret, *The Library Window: A Story of the Seen and Unseen*, Classic Books Library, 2007

Partington, Charles F., *The British Cyclopaedia of Literature, History, Geography, Law and Politics*, Orr and Smith, London, 1836

Taylor, Rev. J. W., *Some Historical Antiquities*, William Robertson, Cupar, 1868

Various, *Descriptive Account of the Principle Towns in Scotland*, Edinburgh, 1828

Various, *The Kingdom of Fife in Days Gone By*, Lang Syne Publishers Ltd, Undated

Weldon, Fay, *Auto Da Fay*, Flamingo, 2009

Whyte-Melville, G.J., *The Queens Maries: A Romance of Holyrood*, Longmans, Green and Co., London, 1871

Wilson, Daniel, *Prehistoric Annals of Scotland*, Macmillan, London, 1863

Woodrow, Robert, *Analecta: Or Materials for a History of Remarkable Providences Volume 1*, Edinburgh Printing Co., 1842

Woodrow, Robert, *Private Letters*, Edinburgh, 1829

Woodrow, Robert, *The History of the Sufferings of the Church of Scotland Volume III*, Blackie Fullarton & Co., 1829

Wynd, Alexander, *History of the Parish Church of the Holy Trinity St Andrews*, Lulu 2012

Magazines

Harrower, Annie, 'The Ancient Ways', in *Scotland Magazine*, Issue 47, October 2009

Harrower, Annie, 'The City of Souls', in *Scotland Magazine*, Issue 50, April 2010

Hayden, Gary, 'St Andrews' Ghosts' in *Scotland Magazine*, Issue 38, April 2008

Sexton, George, ' Bodach Glas' in The *Spiritual Magazine*, Volume 2, 1876

Newspapers

Fife Herald, And Kinross Strathearn, and Clackmannan Advertiser: 15th January 1846, 14th July 1859, 20th February 1868, 2nd July 1868, 11th September 1873.

Press and Journal 8th April 1942.

The Aberdeen Journal 9th February 1894.

The Daily Mail 22nd May 2013

The Daily News: 17th January 1887.

The Daily Record and Mail: 30th October 1916.

The Dundee Advertiser 17th December 1864.

The Dundee Courier: 3rd July 1861, 15th December 1864, 18th April 1895, 7th August 1897, 9th June 1899, 26th May 1900, 16th February 1901, 6th February 1904, 8th February 1904, 15th March 1904, 22nd April 1904, 22nd October 1906, 14th June 1913, 19th May 1915, 15th August 1933, 17th April 1948, 31st May 1950, 16th February 1901, 3rd August 1904, 17th December 1931, 18th August 1933, 18th July 1934, 19th November 1936, 2nd March 1939, 3rd May 1939, 8th March 1940, 24th June 1946, 23rd June 1947.

The Evening News: 15th August 1933.

The Evening Post: 7th October 1902, 5th February 1904, 15th February 1904, 12th May 1964.

The Evening Telegraph: 1st February 1894, 6th August 1897, 30th September 1903, 19th October 1905, 15th July 1915, 5th January 1916, 6th October 1933, 5th March 1938.

The Sunday Post: 26th May 1900, 22nd June 1947.

Websites

Archives Hub: http://archiveshub.ac.uk/data/gb254-ms180

Christianity Today – John Knox: http://www.christianitytoday.com/ch/131christians/denominationalfounders/knox.html?start=2

Deceased Online: https://www.deceasedonline.com/servlet/GSDOSearch?AcctView=Login&SrchView=Basic&DetsView=Content&ListSource=Contributors&section=CONTRIBUTORS&context=SCOTMI&lang=E

Echoes from the Vault: http://standrewsrarebooks.wordpress.com/2013/10/31/special-collections-ghost-tour/

English Bible History – John Knox: http://www.greatsite.com/timeline-english-bible-history/john-knox.html

Historic Scotland: http://www.historic-scotland.gov.uk/

National Library of Scotland: http://www.nls.uk/

Paranormal Database: http://www.paranormaldatabase.com/reports/theatredata.php?pageNum_paradata=3&totalRows_paradata=112

Paranormal Discovery: http://paranormaldiscovery.org/?page_id=171

Parks and Gardens: http://www.parksandgardens.org/places-and-people/site/8206?preview=1

Places of Worship in Scotland: http://www.scottishchurches.org.uk/sites/site/id/4713/name/Franciscan+Friary+%28Greyfriars%29+St+Andrews+and+St+Leonards+Fife

Supernatural St Andrews

Reformation History:
http://reformationhistory.org/presbyterianism.html
Royal Commission on the Ancient and Historical Monuments of Scotland: http://www.rcahms.gov.uk/

Scottish Cinemas and Theatres Project:
http://www.scottishcinemas.org.uk/scotland/standrews/index.html

Scottish Ghosts: http://scottishghosts.webs.com/theatreghosts.htm

Society for Psychical Research: http://www.spr.ac.uk/

St Leonards School: http://www.stleonards-fife.org/our_school/history

The Black Watch: http://www.theblackwatch.co.uk/index/sergeant-john-ripley

The Byre Theatre: http://byretheatre.com/history/

The Hazel tree: http://the-hazel-tree.com/2014/10/17/ghosts-of-st-andrews/

The Inn at Lathones:
http://www.innatlathones.com/Home/History.php?pg=190

The Old Course Hotel: http://www.oldcoursehotel.co.uk/golf/the-dukes

The Sinner: http://www.thesinner.net

The StAndard: https://www.st-andrews.ac.uk/media/press-office/standard/StAndard-Issue17.pdf

University of St Andrews: https://www.st-andrews.ac.uk/visiting/about/history/

Visit St Andrews: http://www.visitstandrews.com/

Wanderings in a Haunted United Kingdom:
http://wanderingsinahauntedkingdom.blogspot.co.uk/2010/07/veiled-nun-of-st-leonards.html

Wikipedia – Archibald Montgomerie:
http://en.wikipedia.org/wiki/Archibald_Montgomerie,_13th_Earl_of_Eglinton

Printed in Great Britain
by Amazon